Alternative Funding Sources

James L. Catanzaro, *Editor*
Triton College

Allen D. Arnold, *Editor*
Triton College

NEW DIRECTIONS FOR COMMUNITY COLLEGES
ARTHUR M. COHEN, *Editor-in-Chief*
FLORENCE B. BRAWER, *Associate Editor*

Number 68, Winter 1989

Paperback sourcebooks in
The Jossey-Bass Higher Education Series

Jossey-Bass Inc., Publishers
San Francisco • Oxford

James L. Catanzaro, Allen D. Arnold (eds.).
Alternative Funding Sources.
New Directions for Community Colleges, no. 68.
Volume XVII, number 4.
San Francisco: Jossey-Bass, 1989.

New Directions for Community Colleges
Arthur M. Cohen, *Editor-in-Chief;* Florence B. Brawer, *Associate Editor*

New Directions for Community Colleges is published quarterly by Jossey-Bass Inc., Publishers (publication number USPS 121-710), in association with the ERIC Clearinghouse for Junior Colleges. *New Directions* is numbered sequentially—please order extra copies by sequential number. The volume and issue numbers above are included for the convenience of libraries. Second-class postage paid at San Francisco, California, and at additional mailing offices. POSTMASTER: Send address changes to Jossey-Bass, Inc., Publishers, 350 Sansome Street, San Francisco, California 94104.

The material in this publication is based on work sponsored wholly or in part by the Office of Educational Research and Improvement, U.S. Department of Education, under contract number RI-88-062002. Its contents do not necessarily reflect the views of the Department, or any other agency of the U.S. Government.

Editorial correspondence should be sent to the Editor-in-Chief, Arthur M. Cohen, at the ERIC Clearinghouse for Junior Colleges, University of California, Los Angeles, California 90024.

Library of Congress Catalog Card Number LC 85-644753

International Standard Serial Number ISSN 0194-3081

International Standard Book Number ISBN 1-55542-843-6

Cover art by WILLI BAUM

Manufactured in the United States of America. Printed on acid-free paper.

Ordering Information

The paperback sourcebooks listed below are published quarterly and can be ordered either by subscription or single copy.
Subscriptions cost $64.00 per year for institutions, agencies, and libraries. Individuals can subscribe at the special rate of $48.00 per year *if payment is by personal check*. (Note that the full rate of $64.00 applies if payment is by institutional check, even if the subscription is designated for an individual.) Standing orders are accepted.
Single copies are available at $14.95 when payment accompanies order. (California, New Jersey, New York, and Washington, D.C., residents please include appropriate sales tax.) For billed orders, cost per copy is $14.95 plus postage and handling.
Substantial discounts are offered to organizations and individuals wishing to purchase bulk quantities of Jossey-Bass sourcebooks. Please inquire.
Please note that these prices are for the calendar year 1989 and are subject to change without notice. Also, some titles may be out of print and therefore not available for sale.
To ensure correct and prompt delivery, all orders must give either the *name of an individual* or an *official purchase order number*. Please submit your order as follows:

Subscriptions: specify series and year subscription is to begin.
Single Copies: specify sourcebook code (such as, CC1) and first two words of title.

Mail all orders to:
Jossey-Bass Inc., Publishers
350 Sansome Street
San Francisco, California 94104

New Directions for Community Colleges Series
Arthur M. Cohen, *Editor-in-Chief*
Florence B. Brawer, *Associate Editor*

CC1 *Toward a Professional Faculty,* Arthur M. Cohen
CC2 *Meeting the Financial Crisis,* John Lombardi
CC3 *Understanding Diverse Students,* Dorothy M. Knoell

CC4   *Updating Occupational Education,* Norman C. Harris
CC5   *Implementing Innovative Instruction,* Roger H. Garrison
CC6   *Coordinating State Systems,* Edmund J. Gleazer, Jr., Roger Yarrington
CC7   *From Class to Mass Learning,* William M. Birenbaum
CC8   *Humanizing Student Services,* Clyde E. Blocker
CC9   *Using Instructional Technology,* George H. Voegel
CC10 *Reforming College Governance,* Richard C. Richardson, Jr.
CC11 *Adjusting to Collective Bargaining,* Richard J. Ernst
CC12 *Merging the Humanities,* Leslie Koltai
CC13 *Changing Managerial Perspectives,* Barry Heermann
CC14 *Reaching Out Through Community Service,* Hope M. Holcomb
CC15 *Enhancing Trustee Effectiveness,* Victoria Dziuba, William Meardy
CC16 *Easing the Transition from Schooling to Work,* Harry F. Silberman, Mark B. Ginsburg
CC17 *Changing Instructional Strategies,* James O. Hammons
CC18 *Assessing Student Academic and Social Progress,* Leonard L. Baird
CC19 *Developing Staff Potential,* Terry O'Banion
CC20 *Improving Relations with the Public,* Louis W. Bender, Benjamin R. Wygal
CC21 *Implementing Community-Based Education,* Ervin L. Harlacher, James F. Gollattscheck
CC22 *Coping with Reduced Resources,* Richard L. Alfred
CC23 *Balancing State and Local Control,* Searle F. Charles
CC24 *Responding to New Missions,* Myron A. Marty
CC25 *Shaping the Curriculum,* Arthur M. Cohen
CC26 *Advancing International Education,* Maxwell C. King, Robert L. Breuder
CC27 *Serving New Populations,* Patricia Ann Walsh
CC28 *Managing in a New Era,* Robert E. Lahti
CC29 *Serving Lifelong Learners,* Barry Heermann, Cheryl Coppeck Enders, Elizabeth Wine
CC30 *Using Part-Time Faculty Effectively,* Michael H. Parsons
CC31 *Teaching the Sciences,* Florence B. Brawer
CC32 *Questioning the Community College Role,* George B. Vaughan
CC33 *Occupational Education Today,* Kathleen F. Arns
CC34 *Women in Community Colleges,* Judith S. Eaton
CC35 *Improving Decision Making,* Mantha Mehallis
CC36 *Marketing the Program,* William A. Keim, Marybelle C. Keim
CC37 *Organization Development: Change Strategies,* James Hammons
CC38 *Institutional Impacts on Campus, Community, and Business Constituencies,* Richard L. Alfred
CC39 *Improving Articulation and Transfer Relationships,* Frederick C. Kintzer
CC40 *General Education in Two-Year Colleges,* B. Lamar Johnson
CC41 *Evaluating Faculty and Staff,* Al Smith
CC42 *Advancing the Liberal Arts,* Stanley F. Turesky
CC43 *Counseling: A Crucial Function for the 1980s,* Alice S. Thurston, William A. Robbins
CC44 *Strategic Management in the Community College,* Gunder A. Myran
CC45 *Designing Programs for Community Groups,* S. V. Martorana, William E. Piland
CC46 *Emerging Roles for Community College Leaders,* Richard L. Alfred, Paul A. Elsner, R. Jan LeCroy, Nancy Armes
CC47 *Microcomputer Applications in Administration and Instruction,* Donald A. Dellow, Lawrence H. Poole

CC48 *Customized Job Training for Business and Industry,* Robert J. Kopecek, Robert G. Clarke
CC49 *Ensuring Effective Governance,* William L. Deegan, James F. Gollattscheck
CC50 *Strengthening Financial Management,* Dale F. Campbell
CC51 *Active Trusteeship for a Changing Era,* Gary Frank Petty
CC52 *Maintaining Institutional Integrity,* Donald E. Puyear, George B. Vaughan
CC53 *Controversies and Decision Making in Difficult Economic Times,* Billie Wright Dziech
CC54 *The Community College and Its Critics,* L. Stephen Zwerling
CC55 *Advances in Instructional Technology,* George H. Voegel
CC56 *Applying Institutional Research,* John Losak
CC57 *Teaching the Developmental Education Student,* Kenneth M. Ahrendt
CC58 *Developing Occupational Programs,* Charles R. Doty
CC59 *Issues in Student Assessment,* Dorothy Bray, Marcia J. Belcher
CC60 *Marketing Strategies for Changing Times,* Wellford W. Wilms, Richard W. Moore
CC61 *Enhancing Articulation and Transfer,* Carolyn Prager
CC62 *Issues in Personnel Management,* Richard I. Miller, Edward W. Holzapfel, Jr.
CC63 *Collaborating with High Schools,* Janet E. Lieberman
CC64 *External Influences on the Curriculum,* David B. Wolf, Mary Lou Zoglin
CC65 *A Search for Institutional Distinctiveness,* Barbara K. Townsend
CC66 *Using Student Tracking Systems Effectively,* Trudy H. Bers
CC67 *Perspectives on Student Development,* William L. Deegan, Terry O'Banion

Contents

Editors' Notes   1
James L. Catanzaro, Allen D. Arnold

1. *The Community College Foundation Today*   5
   A. *History, Characteristics, and Assets*
   Dan Angel, Dale Gares
   B. *Reasons for Success*
   G. Jeremiah Ryan

   Community college foundations have come of age. Proper planning and determined execution under effective leadership can result in significant corporate support.

2. *Foundation Restricted Funds, A Special Application: Miami-Dade's Endowed Teaching Chair*   21
   Horace Jerome Traylor, Stephen G. Katsinas, Siegfried E. Herrmann

   Miami-Dade's remarkably successful transfer of the endowed chair concept from the four-year to the two-year institution has become a national model for other community colleges.

3. *Alumni: Friends and Funds for Your Institution*   29
   Richard J. Pokrass

   Many community colleges are learning that there are long-term paybacks to institutions that make friends of their alumni.

4. *Alternative Education/Alternative Revenue*   35
   A. *Contract Training: Public and Private Sector Models*
   Raymond Lestina, Beverly A. Curry
   B. *Media Technology Begets Revenue*
   Jana B. Kooi

   Contract training not only means additional institutional revenue for community colleges but strengthens important connections with business/industry and public agencies.

5. *Economic Development, the Community College, and Technology Training*   51
   Steve Maradian

   Economic development is tied in most states to the community college's role in training and retraining of employees to meet industry needs.

6. *Entrepreneurship in the Community College:* 57
Revenue Diversification
Richard W. Brightman
An unexpected number of community colleges are increasing revenues by going into business.

7. *A Case for Commercial Development of College Property* 67
Richard W. McDowell, W. Kenneth Lindner
Commercial development of college land requires the deft hand of the college's board of trustees. Schoolcraft College has integrated the public and private sectors compatibly.

8. *Performance Contracting: Profits and Perils* 75
Charles C. Spence, Jeffrey G. Oliver
Higher education, especially at research universities, has long felt the economic impact of grant funds. For the community college, the performance contract may provide an equal opportunity for alternate funding.

Appendix 1. A Guide to Key Resources 85

Appendix 2. Companies that Match to Junior 111
or Community Colleges

Index 121

Editors' Notes

Since the 1970s the search for alternative funding sources has been one of the most distinctive and important endeavors of public two-year colleges. In college after college administrative effort has shifted to the pursuit of new funding, in many cases as a top priority.

The most significant reason for this recent and intense preoccupation with fresh revenue sources is the softening of governmental support for public higher education. Though varying from state to state, federal and state subsidization of public higher education generally has declined, even in the one sector that has displayed the most growth and commitment to societal needs: two-year colleges.

This decline has occurred at a time when the costs of education have been higher than ever. Sagging enrollments in many places have not permitted the scale economies of previous times and have checked the common penchant of community colleges to risk-taking based on confidence that enrollment growth would cover the down side.

The most remarkable expenditure is the cost of setting up and sustaining new academic service programs. Fewer courses can be taught effectively in a standard classroom with the instructor limited to the use of chalk and chalkboard. Technical courses now require equipment and facility outlays well beyond anything that would have been imagined in the 1950s and 1960s. Even liberal arts courses increasingly are taught in specialized environments with expensive hardware and software. Many involve use of the computer; many more rely on film, videotape, and costly learning resources with the paraprofessionals to support them.

At the same time, the burden of large tenured and mature faculties has proved greater than traditional revenues can support. These faculties also find themselves limited by obsolescent equipment and facilities, replacement of which was deferred during the 1980s because of spiraling costs.

These elements—the reduction of public support, high setup costs, salary requirements for a mature faculty, and the need to replace equipment and modernize facilities purchased in the heyday of community colleges (the 1960s and early 1970s)—together have heightened the demand on shrinking resources.

The cost of doing business is not the only source of financial constraint. Society has increased rather than reduced its expectations for community colleges. Community development via local economic development and the rescue of the underclass has, in many states by public policy and in other states by expectation, widened the mission and advanced the financial obligation of colleges.

In large and small institutions across the country, the new mandate has been to identify and tap new sources of funds. This volume presents a series of position papers on the most successful alternative funding ventures. Clearly some are possible only in certain domains and in certain circumstances. The efforts required in each search must also be weighed against the possible gain. Those energies sometimes could have produced more remarkable results if spent on traditional sources. For example, in some districts a new tax initiative or referendum could lead to many times the return of even a most successful foundation or outside business venture.

Nevertheless, the purpose of this sourcebook is to indicate where and how new ventures have aided two-year colleges and to provide a sense of how other institutions might follow in this pursuit. Chapter One discusses the most obvious means of alternative funding: the foundation. The two segments show, first, the current high significance of the foundation in the community college, as well as an overview of its development, and, second, the reasons for its success as patterned in the more successful colleges.

The first segment, by Dan Angel and Dale Gares at Austin Community College, ties together their 1980 and 1987 surveys and provides not only a historical perspective on the foundation in the community college but also a profile of combined assets. Their point is that the community college foundation has come of age, with 1988 combined dollars exceeding a quarter of a billion. They have measured and recorded the success of the community college foundation movement; their article also shares the means by which an individual foundation can judge its own individual success.

The second segment, by G. Jeremiah Ryan, delineates specific strategies community colleges have used successfully to bring in dollars, to the point of including "salable" responses to often-posed objections. Although most of these techniques are common to fund raising in higher education in general, Ryan points to one notable exception.

Chapter Two describes what has surely become the new national model for fund raising for "learning projects" in the community college: Miami-Dade's Endowed Teaching Chair Program. Horace Jerome Traylor, Stephen G. Katsinas, and Siegfried E. Herrmann show the "translation" of a four-year college paradigm into a two-year college concept. This superb idea allows fund-raising efforts to focus on the central mission of the college—excellence in teaching.

In Chapter Three, Richard J. Pokrass brings to community college advancement officers an important insight their four-year counterparts have learned—sometimes the hard way. Funds come from friends. Fund raising must begin as friend raising and provide a benefit to the alumni involved.

Contract training has increased significantly in the past ten years as a means of producing institutional revenues. Chapter Four illustrates an excellent model. The first segment, by Raymond Lestina and Beverly A. Curry, deals with contract training in both the public and private sectors. The second segment, by Jana B. Kooi, deals with numerous media delivery systems, including teleconferencing, Instructional Television Fixed Service (ITFS), and cable networks, and their capabilities for enhancing revenue generation.

Government at both state and local levels has become increasingly interested in joint economic development efforts with two-year colleges because they are the educational institutions best prepared to provide access to technology. Chapter Five, by Steve Maradian, focuses on the fact that in today's high-tech society, economic development is linked to ensuring that local industry possesses the technological know-how to develop the products and services appropriate to improving production and service capabilities.

In Chapter Six, Richard W. Brightman makes a bold argument: a college can increase revenues by going into business. For-profit activities by colleges not only are legal, Brightman points out, but more of them already exist than most of us are aware of.

The traditional revenue sources for the community college have been limited to state appropriations, tuition, and local taxes. Chapter Seven, by Richard W. McDowell and W. Kenneth Lindner, illustrates how the leasing of college land has provided significant additional revenues to Schoolcraft College in Michigan. The issues of whether public land can be used for private commercial enterprise and what role trustees have as holders of the land in public trust are both addressed.

In Chapter Eight, Charles C. Spence and Jeffrey G. Oliver lay the ground rules for ensuring the profitability of that venture. Not only the relative merits and availability of funds are covered but also the risks and the down side of performance contracting versus grants.

Appendixes One and Two, developed by G. Jeremiah Ryan, will serve as excellent information resources: a bibliographic reference guide and a list of companies that match employee gifts to two-year institutions.

The editors are indebted to Sunil Chand, Kim Heintzelman, Carole Jackson, and Debbie Spair for their contributions to this volume.

James L. Catanzaro
Allen D. Arnold
Editors

James L. Catanzaro is president of Triton College, River Grove, Illinois.

Allen D. Arnold is executive vice-president of Triton College.

The Community College Foundation Today

A. History, Characteristics, and Assets

B. Reasons for Success

Community college foundations have come of age, with 1988 combined dollars exceeding a quarter of a billion.

A. History, Characteristics, and Assets

Dan Angel, Dale Gares

Before the late 1970s the community college foundation was an uncommon phenomenon, but by the end of the 1980s it has become commonplace. This decade has witnessed unprecedented foundation successes: in Florida, Miami-Dade Community College received the third largest single gift to any higher education institution in America. In Texas, Midland College Foundation received $600,000 to pay the tuition of 450 high school graduates. Patrick Henry Community College Foundation in Virginia was given $3 million to build a fine arts and community center. In Ohio, the Lakeland College Foundation received a bequest of $1.2 million in land for botanical studies and to serve as a future retreat. Miami-Dade's Foundation accepted a special landscaping maintenance endowment fund (popularly labeled "The Grass Fund") dedicated to the beautification and maintenance of campus grounds. And because of donations, California's Santa Barbara Community College Foundation was able to equip its hotel and restaurant training facility completely.

Clearly, the community college foundation has come of age. According to a comprehensive study (Angel and Gares, 1987), in 1987 America's 1,222 community colleges had at least 649 affiliated foundations with collective assets of over a quarter billion dollars.

Historical Perspective

The first important American educational foundations were established in the late 1800s. Community college foundations came much later, and there is some dispute over the specific details. Degerstedt (1979) reported that just one community college foundation had been incorporated by 1950. Luck and Tolle (1978) noted that there were two community college foundations that were at least forty years old in 1973. Robison (1981) claimed that Long Beach City College records showed that a foundation was organized there in 1922. Nusz (1986) argued that the first program of annual giving started at Midway Junior College in Kentucky as early as 1906.

Regardless of the disagreement about the early foundations, the Angel and Gares survey indicates that by 1987 community colleges of all types and sizes had established foundations. As Figure 1 shows, fully 82 percent (649) of the 793 public and private community colleges reporting claimed to have a foundation, and of those that did not, one-third were considering establishing one. This survey was sent to all 1,222 public and private community colleges; the response rate was 64 percent. Extrapolating from the response data, if they were extended to include institutions that did not respond, the number of foundations could exceed 800, assuming a consistency of pattern.

Figure 1 reveals further that there is a clear relationship between the existence of a foundation and the size of the institution. Of the 144 institutions without a foundation, 123 are relatively small (head-count

Figure 1. Community College Foundations, Fall 1987

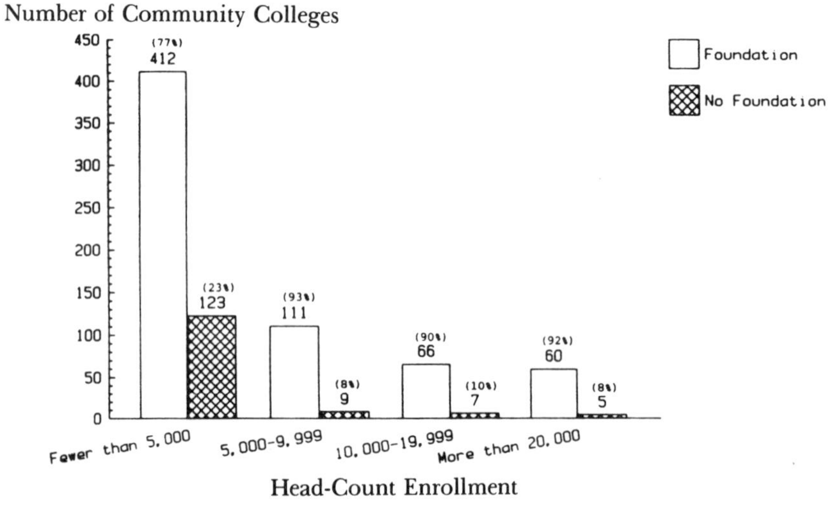

Number of Community Colleges

Head-Count Enrollment	Foundation	No Foundation
Fewer than 5,000	412 (77%)	123 (23%)
5,000–9,999	111 (93%)	9 (8%)
10,000–19,999	66 (90%)	7 (10%)
More than 20,000	60 (92%)	5 (8%)

enrollment fewer than 5,000). In mid-range institutions (5,000 to 9,999), only 9 of the 120 reporting institutions did not have a foundation. At the next institutional level (10,000 to 19,999), only 7 of the 73 institutions had no formal fund-raising operation. Finally, in the large community college category (enrollment over 20,000), just 5 of the reporting 65 institutions had no foundation.

Figure 2 provides a graphic representation of foundation maturity, indicating that of the schools that responded, only sixty-four had foundations before 1966. Community college foundations appear to have been encouraged by the 1965 Higher Education Act, which often offered federal funds for grants and contract competitions with a match requirement. About the same time, Internal Revenue Service tax-exemption rulings began to stimulate giving. Of course, the phenomenal growth in the number of community colleges in the late 1960s and early 1970s translated naturally into more foundations. The most compelling cause, however, seems to have been the decline in public funds over the past two decades. That decline has led to a search for other revenue sources, particularly in states that have seen a steady increase in tuition and fees (the national average was $287 in 1974, $464 in 1980, and $642 in 1987). Pressure on boards and administrators to find relief has spawned private fund drives in community colleges and public universities.

The net effect of these factors was a bull market for community college foundations in the 1970s and 1980s. It is no surprise, then, that 83

Figure 2. How Long Foundations Have Been in Existence

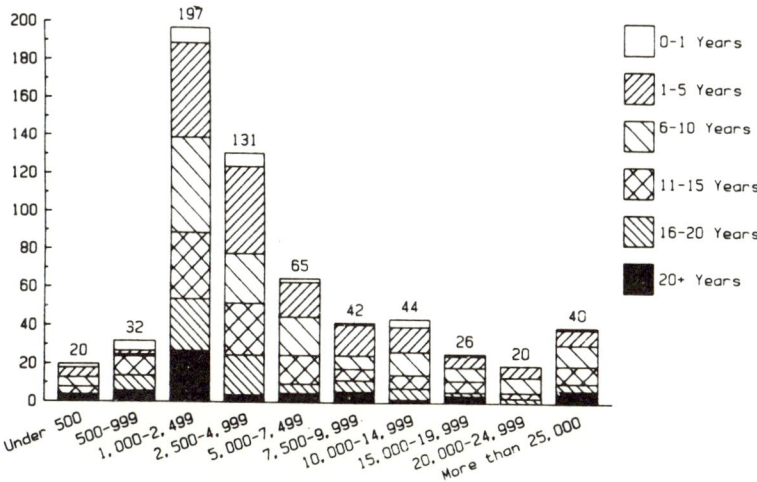

Head-Count Enrollment

were established between 1966 and 1970, 122 between 1971 and 1975, 154 between 1976 and 1980, and 220 between 1981 and 1987 (Angel and Gares, 1987).

Asset Growth

Luck and Tolle (1978) presented the first comprehensive look at foundation assets. Of the 192 foundations they studied, over half had assets of less than $25,000. Angel and Gares (1981) found that total foundation assets were growing rapidly. They noted that 31 percent of community college foundations had assets of more than $100,000 in 1980, while 11 percent had more than $500,000. Seven percent had more than $1 million. Crowson (1985) found that of the 185 foundations providing data, 40 percent had assets between $100,000 and $500,000 and 26 percent had assets over $500,000. The Angel and Gares (1987) Comprehensive Survey (summarized in Figure 3) shows a remarkable gain in total assets as 84 foundations reported assets of more than $1 million each.

Angel and Gares (1981) calculated aggregate minimum, maximum, and average dollar assets in community college foundation coffers. It reported that minimum projections accounted for some $44 million; max-

Figure 3. Community College Foundation Assets, Fall 1987

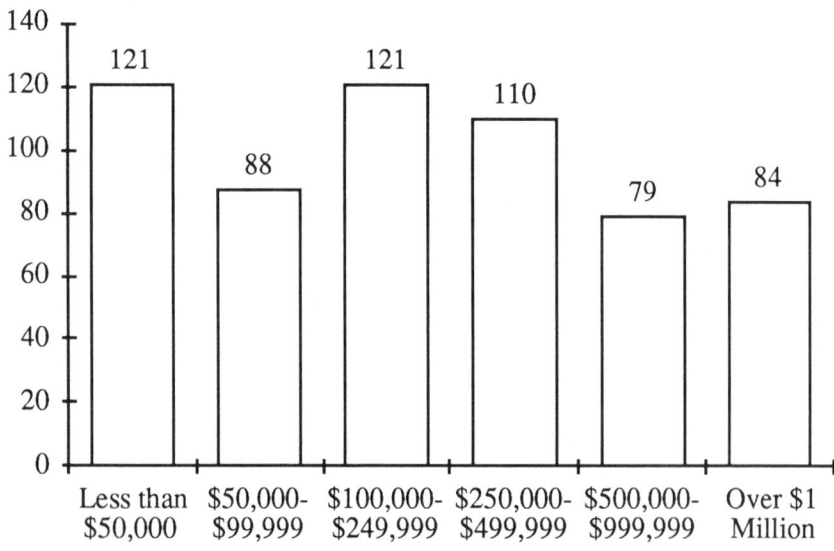

imum projections would allow for $86 million; and the average figure for the all-community-colleges aggregate would be $65 million.

In just seven years the numbers jumped dramatically. By the same methodology, the minimum aggregate assets in community college foundations in 1987 were $167 million, $123 million greater than in 1980. The maximum rose from $86 million to $349 million, while the average increased from $65 million to $258 million. Therefore, it seems safe to say that community college foundation assets in 1988 totaled more than a quarter of a billion dollars. By the late 1980s, private source funding is a demonstrated success.

Establishing a Foundation

How foundations are established and funds collected has been described by a number of authors. Graham (1983) presents a ten-step process; Duffy (1980) identifies seven steps; Hollingsworth (1983) speaks of five phases of development; Sharron (1982) refers to three; Reilley (1985) provides a tome on the topic; and Walters (1987, p. 1) refers to a "three-legged stool."

Perhaps the most useful, because it is inclusive, is Wattenbarger's (1982, p. 27) "typical evolution process," a ten-step format. The process can be summarized as follows: (1) formulate the case statement; (2) describe educational needs in community terms; (3) identify inhabitant factors; (4) analyze the attack; (5) outline needed resources; (6) analyze potential sources of support; (7) establish priorities; (8) develop a foundation program that fits with the college's plans; (9) demonstrate that fit; and (10) evaluate college, community, and foundation activities to ensure that steps 1 through 9 are faithfully followed. This approach appears to be commonly adopted and successful.

Measuring Success

Most analysts seem to agree on a number of key ingredients for success. A first step is to overcome the myths of foundation development. Sharron (1982) presents eight such myths: (1) people will not give to a local tax-supported institution; (2) people will not donate because the educational content is suspect; (3) people will not give because of the constituency of community colleges; (4) people will not give because the community college is seen as an extension of K–12; (5) community colleges do not have adequate prestige to attract contributions; (6) when giving, alumni first think of the four-year college they attended; (7) adequate foundation staffing is usually not available or is too costly to do the job; and (8) the college president is too busy to be effectively involved.

Reversing these eight myths is a good way to pinpoint what it takes to be successful. Each myth must be specifically dealt with before the potential donor is solicited. Complete success depends on such things as a commitment from the entire board of trustees; a strong foundation board to lead the way, supported by the college trustees; a concise and compelling case statement associated with the college's needs; an effective program of community relations already in place; a vigorous special project campaign; an award program to recognize outstanding donors; and full and public accountability. When these requirements are met, appeals can be made to qualified potential donors: area residents, corporations, private foundations, employees, alumni, members of advisory committees, and so forth. These appeals come through annual giving campaigns, memorial giving, and even planned giving programs. Special efforts can be made for capital projects or special programming as well.

Active Versus Passive

The vitality of existing foundations is of interest. Hollingsworth (1983) noted that the 546 foundations she examined fell into two categories: active and inactive. Explaining the latter, Robison (1981) found that many foundations were "set up to receive funds rather than to actively seek them" (p. 24). In fact, Sharron (1982) estimated that only about fifty two-year public institutions in 1982 had aggressive foundation operations. Glandon (1987) made one of the most thorough evaluations of the active/passive dichotomy. He identified 227 colleges having "active" foundations. Of these he found that 107 had achieved "low success" (raised less than $50,000) in 1985, and 120 had "high success" (raised more than $50,000).

Although one may question whether an annual revenue of $50,000 is the best criterion for success, or even a significant criterion, in view of fund-raising costs, there is no doubt that a valid distinction can and should be made between active and passive foundations. According to Angel and Gares's (1987) survey, the community college foundation movement is fast becoming dominated by active-status foundations.

A Revitalization Case

Citrus College, located in the suburbs of Los Angeles, provides a good case study of a foundation's passage from passive to active status (Rasmussen, 1986). The Citrus College Foundation was established officially in 1966. Fifteen years later, in June 1981, this 10,000-student campus could show total foundation assets of only $38,000. "It was strictly a receiving organization," says the foundation's first executive director (p. 39). But 1981 was a difficult time for Citrus College because the effects of California's Proposition 13 were beginning to be felt. The board and new president decided to activate the foundation to see if they could make up some of the anticipated shortfall.

They set out to assemble a strong foundation board made up of community leaders who traveled in moneyed circles. In discussions with leaders on and off campus, two prominent citizens were mentioned: the founder of a worldwide manufacturing corporation and a well-known area resident who had a history of involvement with the college and was himself a man of means. These two key players were approached through close associates. The latter was immediately interested. By chance, the scheduled contact with the former conflicted with an accreditation team visitation. The new college president was torn between the two appointments, so he attempted to keep both. Arriving some twenty minutes late for the luncheon with his foundation prospect, the somewhat apologetic president explained that he had been delayed by the accreditation visit. That remark drew a rather unexpected response: "You mean you left the accreditation team just to come and visit with me?" The president nodded. "Well, if it's that important, then I will serve on your foundation board" (Rasmussen, 1986, p. 39).

With two key members secured, other powerful community leaders rallied to the cause. During the next few months, the newly formed board discovered that prominent people knew there was a community college in the area, but did not know what the school was doing or that it needed direct support. Most of the early work at Citrus dealt with organization and campaign preparation: developing the argument; writing the literature; and planning, planning, planning.

Finally, contacts with potential donors on and off campus began: $100,000 was raised in one hundred days, and $200,000 more during the foundation's second year. The foundation also participated in a voluntary tuition campaign known as "Save Our Community College." Students at the college were asked to contribute money to help the college in the wake of Proposition 13 losses, and the foundation matched the amount contributed by students. Although some doubted whether such an effort would work, a $50,000 goal was established for student contributions. The goal was exceeded and it was matched with $50,000 from outside donors.

The point was made: foundations of two-year colleges can raise significant amounts of additional revenue when there is proper planning and determined execution under effective leadership.

References

Angel, D., and Gares, D. "A Bull Market for Foundations." *Community and Junior College Journal,* 1981, *52,* 5-6.
Crowson, J. "Boards of Directors of Community College Foundations: Charac-

teristics, Roles, and Success." Unpublished doctoral dissertation, University of Mississippi, 1985.

Degerstedt, L. M. "Non-Profit Foundations Formed by Public Community Colleges: Profile of Their Use for External Funding." Doctoral dissertation, Brigham Young University, 1979.

Duffy, E. F. "Characteristics and Conditions of a Successful Community College Foundation." Washington, D.C.: National Council for Resource Development, 1980. (ED 203 918)

Glandon, B. L. "Critical Components of Successful Two-Year College Foundations." Unpublished doctoral dissertation, Brigham Young University, 1987.

Graham, F. R. *New River Community College Educational Foundation, Inc.* Dublin, Virginia: New River Community College, 1983. (ED 283 457)

Hollingsworth, P. "An Investigation of Characteristics of Successful Community College Foundations." Graduate seminar paper, Pepperdine University, 1983. (ED 233 756)

Luck, M. F., and Tolle, D. J. *Community College Development.* Newkirk, 1978.

Nusz, P. J. "Development of Foundation Guidelines." Unpublished doctoral dissertation, Nova University, 1986.

Rasmussen, P. "Citrus College Foundation." *The Glendoran,* 1986, 38-42.

Reilley, T. A. "Raising Money Through an Institutionally Related Foundation." Washington, D.C.: Council for the Advancement and Support of Education, 1985. (ED 256 198)

Robison, S. "The Sky's the Limit." *Community and Junior College Journal,* 1981, 52 (3), 24-26.

Sharron, W. H., Jr. *The Community College Foundation.* Washington, D.C.: National Council for Resource Development, 1982.

Walters, L. "Dollars Equal to the Margin of Excellence." Southern Association of Community and Junior Colleges Occasional Paper, 1987, 5 (2). (ED 281 600)

Wattenbarger, J. L. "The Case for the Community College Foundation." In W. H. Sharron, Jr. (ed.), *The Community College Foundation.* Washington, D.C.: National Council for Resource Development, 1982.

Dan Angel is president and Dale Gares is associate vice-president for academic affairs at Austin Community College, Austin, Texas. They have collaborated previously on both the 1981 and 1987 research surveys on the status of foundations in the community college.

Community colleges have successfully used professional advancement officers to attract significant corporate dollars.

B.
Reasons for Success

G. Jeremiah Ryan

As the Angel and Gares chapter points out, public community colleges are rushing to find additional financial support from the private sector. Their success, although to this point modest compared to the total moneys gained in educational advancement, has nonetheless contributed to the phenomenon that public colleges in the United States now raise more funds from the private sector than do private colleges.

The level of this achievement has surprised the advancement community at large and amazed even the presidents of the recipient colleges. It is in large part the result of community college foundations' having come to terms with the ground rules of private-sector solicitation. One significant step toward this point was taken in 1981 when the National Council for Resource Development commissioned W. Harvey Sharron, Jr., to edit a book that to this day serves as a primer for community colleges wishing to establish a foundation (Sharron, 1982).

How is it that the community college advancement teams translated Sharron's guidelines into strategies that could bring such overwhelming success? The answer has not been immediately apparent. With this question in mind, the Council for the Advancement and Support of Education (CASE) established a research team to approach successful community college fund raisers in 1986 and again in 1987 to identify the elements individual colleges used to solicit corporate donations. The report of that study (Ryan and Smith, 1987) indicated two remarkable similarities. One, there is a striking similarity in the individual schools' approaches to fund raising. Second, although this was not surprising to those who had experience with fund-raising efforts, there is also a marked similarity between what works best for community colleges and what appears to have been working best for some time for successful private and public colleges and universities.

Elements of the Study

The researchers for the project were John Hall, vice-president, CASE; Nanette Smith, vice-president for development at Edison Community College (Florida); and G. Jeremiah Ryan, vice-president for institutional advancement at Monroe Community College (New York). In this study, development officers at selected community colleges that were highly successful in fund-raising activities were contacted and asked the same nine questions:

1. What factors contributed to the college's success?
2. Is there a chief development officer? To whom does the individual report?
3. What solicitation publications were distributed?
4. What solicitation programs were sponsored?
5. What other personnel, if any, exist to support the following development activities:
   a. annual fund
   b. alumni solicitation
   c. corporate solicitation
   d. foundation solicitation
6. What is the time commitment to private fund-raising development of the chief executive?
7. What is the time and financial commitment of the college's board of trustees?
8. What is the time and financial commitment of the college's and foundation's board of directors?
9. What organizational changes will be needed to increase success?

Patterns of Success

The research team found the development officers eager to share their experiences, and the original nine questions quickly proved to be only the start of lengthy telephone interviews that yielded helpful insights. The respondents reported that the transition from failure to success commonly required three changes: (1) an exceptional commitment by the chief executive; (2) a full-time person, with sufficient rank in the institution to get people's notice, to manage the development effort; and (3) the adoption of the "spend money to make money" approach.

Figure 1 shows the relative significance of the factors credited with a foundation's successful soliciting of private sector funds.

Suggested Organizational Changes

The team also found in this interview that certain organizational changes were consistently recommended as a means to increasing the effectiveness of the college's fund-raising efforts. Of those reported (Figure 2), the chief development officers said that adequate support staff to serve the fund-raising process was the most important.

A Notable Exception to the Rule

It was particularly noteworthy that the factors the team found that could be credited with most of the success of fund-raising programs (Figure 1) could as easily have been reported by the development officers at

Figure 1. Factors Credited with Success of Colleges' Advancement Programs

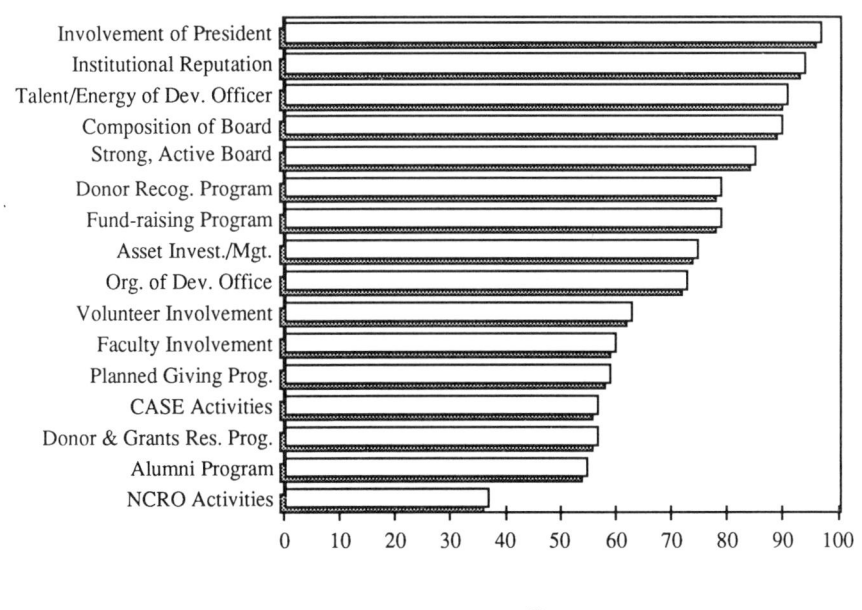

Source: Adapted from Smith, 1986, p. 14.

Figure 2. Organizational Changes Needed to Improve Effectiveness of Advancement Office

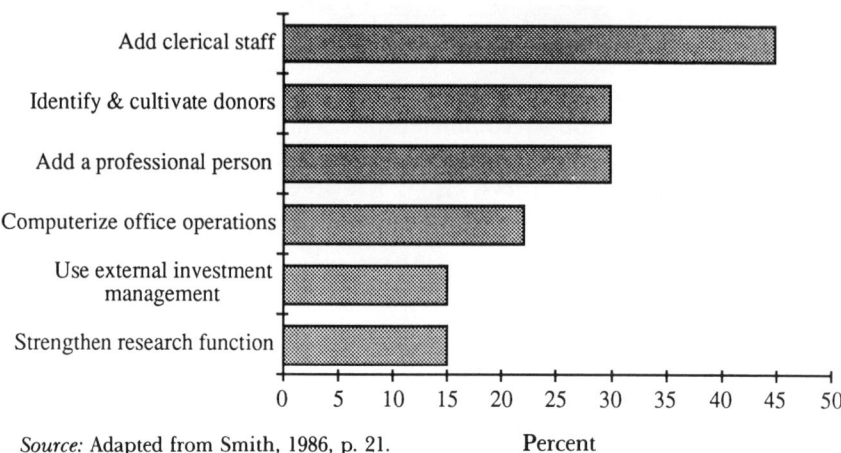

Source: Adapted from Smith, 1986, p. 21.

traditional public or private four-year institutions. There was one significant exception: trustees in community colleges, whether elected or politically appointed, are not active participants in the fund-raising process. This factor is so important that it affects the organizational structure of the foundation itself. In community colleges separate foundations with their own directors are prevalent.

Recommendations of the Team

The study yielded information that confirmed that good organization, leadership, and resource commitment are essential if fund raising is to be successful. Specifically, the respondents told the research team:
1. Few foundations were successful in early efforts.
2. The "spend money to make money" approach is necessary for success.
3. The rich will get richer.
4. The president's involvement is necessary for success and crucial for excellence.
5. Many foundation boards are in transition from inactive to active.
6. The existence of a full-time development person with an office is essential for success.
7. College trustees are not active fund raisers and probably will not become so.

In sum, what it takes to make a successful community college fund-raising program is to adapt a traditional organization and implement a traditional approach.

Figure 3. Overcoming Public Skepticism

Question	Response
Why do public institutions of higher learning need private-sector funding?	The moneys received from state and federal funding are insufficient for capital improvements necessary to train first-rate employees in the technologies in which state-of-the-art equipment changes rapidly.
Why are additional facilities and equipment needed?	State-of-the-art equipment and facilities are needed to keep pace with rapidly developing technology in business and science. Student access to computers is a growing requirement, as is the separation of academic and administrative computer needs.
Why do low-cost community colleges need scholarship funds?	The community college population is diverse: recent high school graduates; older adults, including returning women; workers updating skills; and handicapped students. Recent federal and state reductions in student assistance underscore the need for additional sources of revenue. In this situation, the groups mentioned need financial aid more than would be expected of a more homogeneous population.
How will funds for faculty enrichment provide opportunities?	Special leaves are needed for studying new disciplines; for exchanges with business and industry that allow faculty to gain related work experience; for special faculty projects in research, curriculum development, and retraining; and for recognition of excellence in teaching through endowed chairs.
How do members of the board of directors help the foundation?	Through activities such as developing fund-raising strategies and priorities; participating at foundation meetings and special events; identifying, cultivating and soliciting corporate, individual, and foundation prospects; and managing and disbursing foundation funds.

Resource Guide to Case Preparation

The survey respondents frequently reported that when they began their efforts there had been considerable public skepticism about a publicly financed community college's entry into private resource development. Some typical questions and responses are provided in Figure 3 for the reader's use in preparing his or her own case.

References

Ryan, G. J., and Smith, N. J. "Characteristics of Excellence in Community College Fund Raising." Paper presented at 67th annual convention of the American Association of Community and Junior Colleges, Dallas, Tex., April 1987.

Sharron, W. H., Jr. *The Community College Foundation.* Washington, D.C.: National Council for Resource Development, 1982.

Smith, N. J. "Organizational Models of Successful Advancement Programs." Paper presented at the Annual Conference on Advancing Two-Year Institutions of the Council for the Advancement and Support of Education, Alexandria, Va., December 9-11, 1986.

G. Jeremiah Ryan is vice-president for institutional advancement at Monroe Community College, Rochester, New York. As an AACJC Fellow in 1988, he made considerable contributions to the literature available on community college foundations.

Miami-Dade has a consistently high track record in soliciting corporate donations. Their most recent approach, which transfers the endowed chair concept from the four-year to the two-year institution, has been remarkably successful and has become a national model for other community colleges.

Foundation Restricted Funds, a Special Application: Miami-Dade's Endowed Teaching Chair

Horace Jerome Traylor, Stephen G. Katsinas, Siegfried E. Herrmann

Distinguished Professors Concept

The distinguished professorship has long been a tradition at many universities. It is most often used to lure eminent researchers to college campuses, typically at a cost of $1 million per chair. The Endowed Teaching Chair Program at Miami-Dade Community College takes that tradition and molds it to the requirements of the community college. The more modest sum of $75,000 per chair is required to generate roughly $7,500 per year in discretionary funds to be awarded to teaching faculty who have already distinguished themselves in the classroom. Through the use of the Florida Academic Improvement Trust Fund (FAITF), a state "eminent scholars" endowment match program for public community college foundations, a $45,000 private contribution creates a $30,000 state match (60-40 basis).

The FAITF program is discussed below in detail along with the operational strategy employed by Miami-Dade Community College's institutional advancement office to endow 100 teaching chairs over three years.

The concept of endowed teaching chairs is new to community colleges, even though teaching is at the center of the mission of the American community college. The program at Miami-Dade is intended to stimulate and honor teaching excellence. To understand why and how Miami-Dade Community College developed the Endowed Teaching Chair Program, it is necessary to understand the history of fund raising at the college, its philosophy of external funding, and the Teaching/Learning Project of which the Endowed Teaching Chair Program is an integral part.

Development at Miami-Dade

The development function at Miami-Dade, as at most community colleges, is relatively new, having been established in the late 1960s following the passage of the landmark Higher Education Act of 1965 (Keener, 1982). The Miami-Dade Community College Foundation grew in prominence as the college examined and adopted portions of the university private fund-raising model. Keener (1982) specifically cites the importance of "integration of institutional external resources with defined pursuits of the College."

At Miami-Dade Community College the following philosophy of fund raising has evolved: the institutional advancement office believes that a direct-support, nonprofit foundation attached to an institution of higher education is most successful when a public-spirited group of citizens understands the central mission of the college, is in agreement with it, and can articulate it to the business and civic community. The Miami-Dade Community College Foundation, therefore, has two key functions: (1) to manage and administer the various gifts made according to the wishes of the donor consistent with foundation policy and procedure regarding acceptance of gifts and (2) to raise additional dollars in support of the institution. Of these two functions, the first is more important than the second: people make major gifts to charitable organizations in which they trust that the dollars they worked so hard to earn will be managed with the same care required to create such wealth. If there is a *perception* that the community college will manage a donor's gift better than other charitable repositories, the donations will come forth. If that perception does not exist in the minds of potential donors, a development campaign is doomed to failure.

For a community college fund-raising campaign to succeed, therefore, it must be rooted, as Wattenbarger (1982) and others have noted, in the mission of the institution. The role of staff, including the development office and the president's office, is to empower the foundation board of directors to articulate to the business community how that specific gift will make a qualitative difference. To accomplish this, the foundation must be involved in and informed about the strategic planning process of the college. This has long been the case at Miami-Dade.

The Teaching/Learning Project

The Endowed Teaching Chair Program fits into the Miami-Dade Teaching/Learning Project and demonstrates that the institutional advancement function is integrated into the college's long- and short-term planning. A 1975 study of the college's general education requirements made it clear that the critical issue facing Miami-Dade was the declining academic skills of its entering students. A series of systemic changes were initiated, funded in part by a substantial Department of Education Title III Strengthening Developing Institutions grant. The key elements of the 1975 reforms included mandatory entrance testing and placement, the "Academic Alert" early warning and related systems for improving the speed and quality of communication with students, and prescriptive advisement. These major reforms were cited by community college researchers Roueche and Baker (1987).

It has been estimated that one-third of the college's faculty will retire during the late 1980s and early 1990s. This fact has provided the college with a tremendous opportunity in three important areas: (1) hiring a faculty consistent with Miami's dynamic multicultural demography (approximately 40 percent Anglo, 40 percent Hispanic, 20 percent black); (2) developing a system of professional faculty development that will help new professors learn what experienced professors already know about teaching students who often are underprepared academically (especially important in view of the differences between student populations in a typical state flagship, a private research university, and the community college); (3) developing a new evaluation, hiring, and reward system that will improve classroom teaching by new faculty as well as existing faculty. Thus rewarding outstanding teaching was seen as the best way to place teaching at its rightful center of the community college mission. Baker sees the Teaching/Learning Project as the inevitable next step for Miami-Dade: "They've gotten the curriculum straightened out; they've got support systems in place to help students through the institution; now they've got to help the classroom teacher" (Heller, 1988, p. 13).

There are three major goals of the Teaching/Learning Program:
1. To improve the quality of teaching and learning at Miami-Dade.
2. To make teaching at Miami-Dade a professionally rewarding career.
3. To make teaching and learning the focal point of college activities and decision-making processes.

The *Teaching/Learning Project 1986-87 Summary Report* (1987) demonstrated how the institutional advancement function was integrated into the college's program planning process. The following key project elements were named:

> Creation of subcommittees to address the issues that will ensure institutionalization of the outcome of the Teaching/Learning Project, e.g., changes in the way tenure is granted; modifications of the evaluation and promotion system for teaching faculty, support personnel and academic administrators, among others.
>
> A focus on mechanisms by which teachers can get feedback on their teaching and creation of a support system to strengthen their skills and knowledge of instructional delivery.
>
> Implementation of an Endowed Teaching Chair Program as one means of recognizing outstanding faculty.
>
> Exploration of the "learning" side of teaching/learning relationship (how students learn).
>
> Provision for participation in the Project for those not on the Steering Committee or its Subcommittees (e.g., retreats, open meetings).
>
> Opportunity for interaction with external consultants and with colleges across M-DCC campuses around matters of vital educational concern.
>
> Linkages with other institutions having similar teaching/learning goals.
>
> Tangible recognition of the learning environment as the central focus of college operations (through enhanced support services to teaching faculty, upgraded classrooms, shifts in priorities for decision making).

The Endowed Teaching Chair Program is a $10 million, three-year fund-raising campaign to endow 100 chairs for outstanding teaching faculty and to produce an additional $2.5 million in scholarship and program support. The funds are allocated according to the following formula: $5,000 in a salary supplement and $2,500 for the discretionary use of the professor awarded the chair, related to the academic teaching area.

Planning and Organizing the Campaign

There are four key elements to the strategic plan on which the Endowed Teaching Chair Program has been based:

1. Channeling the volunteer support developed in the $5,000 "Margin of Excellence Endowment Campaign" directly into the Endowed Teaching Chair Program.
2. Involving the institutional leadership, particularly the college president and the four campus vice-presidents (campus chief executive officers), in the fund-raising efforts.
3. Recruiting dynamic leadership, especially from the foundation board of directors, to lead the campaign.
4. Providing as many attractive methods for donor participation as practicable.
5. Involving the foundation board of directors as much as possible in all aspects of campaign planning and execution.

It was our desire as institutional advancement professionals to structure the campaign for success and to maintain and build on an existing base of grass-roots volunteers. Responsibilities were clearly defined, and two dynamic foundation board members, Louis Wolfson III and Andrew S. Blank, agreed to cochair the Endowed Teaching Chair campaign. They each agreed personally to endow a chair and through their professional and business contacts, to identify and attract a total of five chairs over a three-year period. Each of the other twenty-two members of the board were asked either to endow or to assist in identifying and attracting a chair, an effort that would produce an estimated twenty chairs (and would be reinforced by the leadership of the campaign cochairs and the support of the chairman of the board of directors, Martin Fine, and the chairman of the Miami-Dade Community College District board of trustees, Daniel Gill). The Miami-Dade foundation board of directors has twenty-five members, including all seven of the district trustees, who are appointed by the governor of Florida and confirmed by the Florida cabinet, the chief executive officer of the college, Robert H. McCabe, and seventeen elected directors from the business and community of Dade County. Of the twenty-five board members, roughly one-half served on the college district board of trustees at one time or are graduates of the institution. College president Robert H. McCabe agreed to attract ten chairs, and each of the four campus vice-presidents agreed to attract a minimum of five chairs, for a combined total of thirty.

The foundation's chief of protocol, Peter C. Clayton, agreed to take the leadership in promoting the Willing Founders Program. This program makes it possible for a person fifty-five or older to endow a chair with a bequest of $75,000. Because value is received—the chair is made operational as soon as possible by the commitment of dollars from the college's auxiliary services funds, such as vending machines and bookstore revenues—the contractual legal effect is quite solid. The Willing Founders Program gives potential donors another opportunity to participate through either a charitable remainder trust created during the donor's lifetime or a bequest. It is expected that the Willing Founders Program will produce twenty chairs over three years, thanks in large part to the strong, able leadership of Peter Clayton, who has been provided an office and staff support in the institutional advancement quarters. Clayton agreed to take the volunteer leadership for this program only after the foundation board of directors agreed to double his annual salary to $2 per year.

Thus, by the end of June 1990, we expect that eighty chairs will be identified and attracted through structured efforts mentioned above. Another structure for success is the President's Blue Ribbon Committee, consisting of corporate and civic leaders of Dade County. Each of these leaders agreed to endow a chair and to attract an additional chair over the three-year life of the program. To create the Blue Ribbon Committee, solicitations on behalf of President McCabe were made by institutional advancement staff.

Although the commitments to establish the chair and structure the campaign were completed by December 1987, the formal campaign did not kick off until June 7, 1988. This six-month period was critical to obtaining the commitments of those serving on the President's Blue Ribbon Committee to endow a quarter of the teaching chairs before the program was officially announced. Other community colleges considering development programs are strongly advised to delay the official announcement of the campaign until at least one-quarter of the commitments needed to obtain success are in hand. This strategy creates the perception of success, which is critical to institutions seeking private-sector contributions.

Motivating Contributors

What motivates individuals to contribute to a community college? At the top of the list one would likely find the belief that the institution represents quality, support for the community college's mission, and understanding of the community college's vital role in contributing to the educational, cultural, and economic well-being of its service area. For community colleges to succeed in private fund raising, it is essential that the same promotional facts presented to the state legislature be forthrightly communicated to business leaders. Time after time, institutional advancement staff found genuine interest among the business community in the "access with opportunity" mission of the community college. The roster of supporters present at the Endowed Teaching Chair campaign kick-off luncheon looked like a corporate and professional "Who's Who" of South Florida. In other words, the community college and its uplifting mission are great selling points.

The Endowed Teaching Chair Program dramatically recognizes the commitment of the college to attracting and retaining outstanding faculty with demonstrated teaching excellence. It will be a recruitment tool of inestimable value at a critical juncture in the history of Miami-Dade Community College. Fifty percent of the college's full-time faculty will reach retirement age over the next five to seven years. The Endowed Teaching Chair Program addresses a vital need of the college as it prepares students for success in the twenty-first century.

References

Heller, S. "Miami-Dade College Begins Project to Bolster Teaching by Evaluating New Professors and Rewarding Classroom Performance." *Chronicle of Higher Education*, 1988, *34* (31), 12-13, 18.

Keener, B. J. "The Foundation's Role in Resource Development." In W. H. Sharron, Jr. (ed.), *The Community College Foundation*. Washington, D.C.: National Council for Resource Development, 1982.

Roueche, J. E., and Baker, G. A., III. *Access and Excellence: The Open Door College*. Washington, D.C.: Community College Press, 1987.

Teaching/Learning Project 1986-87 Summary Report (Year One). Poster. Miami, Fla.: Miami-Dade Community College, 1987.

Wattenbarger, J. L. "The Case for the Community College Foundation." In W. H. Sharron, Jr. (ed.), *The Community College Foundation*. Washington, D.C.: National Council for Resource Development, 1982.

Horace Jerome Traylor is vice-president for institutional advancement and president of the Miami-Dade Community College Foundation.

Stephen G. Katsinas is associate director of institutional advancement at Miami-Dade Community College.

Siegfried E. Herrmann is director of development at Miami-Dade Community College.

Interest in alumni relations at public community colleges is relatively new. But many colleges are learning there are long-term paybacks to institutions that make friends of their alumni.

Alumni: Friends and Funds for Your Institution

Richard J. Pokrass

A solid alumni relations program is the cornerstone of institutional advancement efforts at most four-year colleges and universities throughout the United States. The *Handbook of Institutional Advancement* (Rowland, 1986) devotes twelve chapters to the development of alumni relations. Alumni serve as a valuable resource in fund raising, student recruitment, job placement, and volunteer programs.

Yet until recently little emphasis has been placed on alumni relations at two-year colleges, especially public community colleges. The reasons are twofold. First, because of the relative youth of the community colleges—most are now in only their third or fourth decade of operation—administrators and faculty often felt their alumni were not sufficiently well established in their respective careers or highly placed in the "system" to be of benefit to the institution. A second and closely related factor is an insufficient understanding of all that a sound alumni program can accomplish for an institution.

As more two-year colleges have, in the past decade, either established or examined the benefits of alumni associations, many have done so with only one thought: money. They have seen colleges and universities raise hundreds of thousands, even millions, of dollars from alumni to endow faculty chairs, to fund new facilities, to provide the difference between ordinary programs and truly superb ones. A word of caution: these community college advancement types, with their new-found desire to pursue perceived riches, need to remember that the first step to getting donations is building friendships. Most of the four-year colleges and universities that have long-term success with their alumni programs have learned the concept of mutual benefits: the institution provides something of value to the alumni that makes them want to support their alma mater.

With this point in mind, I suggest that a successful two-year college alumni program, especially in its early years, should not be based on fund raising at all, but rather on friend raising. Financial contributions will come later, the result of those other actions that carefully nurture alumni.

Among the common friend-raising activities are free job placement services, free use of college facilities, discounts to campus events, newsletters and magazines highlighting college happenings and alumni activities, and programs that recognize graduates' personal and professional achievements. None of these activities need be costly to the institution, yet they are of immense interest and value to alumni. The job placement services and free use of facilities are especially useful to young alumni with limited financial resources.

It is equally important to make alumni feel that they are still an important part of the college. A vital step is formally to establish an alumni association. Alumni can serve as officers or members of committees, work directly with the college staff, and feel that they are providing important input into the institution's future success. A formal organization is the centerpiece of a successful two-year college alumni program, especially if the organization enjoys some independence from the college's main administrative structure. Many alumni are in an excellent position to advise the college staff on key issues. In addition, they want to have some say in the destiny of their association. Thus many two-year college alumni groups, with the support of their colleges, have pursued incorporation.

Incorporation gives the alumni group a formal structure, greater credibility in the eyes of some alumni, and in many cases, protection from lawsuits against individual officers. Some colleges, however, choose not to pursue this avenue.

Whether or not an alumni program is officially incorporated, the basics of alumni relations remain the same: focused goals and objectives, effective volunteers, reliable avenues of communication with the host college, and a source of operating funds.

The first of these tasks, establishing appropriate goals and objectives, is vitally important to an alumni association. These objectives must never be inconsistent with those of the host institution: such inconsistencies create counterproductive antagonisms between influential alumni and the college staff and trustees.

The structure of the alumni program is an important component of the alumni relations process. Many two-year college alumni programs are highly centralized, with a strong general alumni association and perhaps a few specialized clubs within the association. Some colleges, however, have opted for the reverse—several specialized alumni clubs with a deliberately weak central governing body or perhaps no general alumni association at all. Whereas alumni clubs at major universities often have a regional basis or reflect the college one attended within the university, two-year college alumni clubs are typically established along the lines of academic majors (engineering, allied health, communications, and so forth) or specific interests (such as athletics or student honors groups). Each college must decide which model is best for its unique situation.

Closely related to the alumni program's structure is the question of which administrative department, if any, will be responsible for coordinating alumni relations and providing the staff support for the alumni association. Since most two-year colleges have not traditionally assigned significant resources to alumni programs, only a small fraction have full-time alumni officers. Alumni programming has usually been assigned as an appendix to departments with many other duties. Some colleges view alumni primarily as a source of revenue and assign alumni responsibilities to the development staff. But there are several other models that have successfully met colleges' needs.

The most common, other than the development model, is to tie in alumni relations with the public relations/public information/college relations function. Schools that have pursued this avenue have generally done so to emphasize, at least initially, two-way communication between alumni and the college. The public relations office is well equipped to keep alumni abreast of ongoing college activities, to seek alumni input on key issues, and even to utilize alumni success stories in advertising and promotional activities.

Four-year colleges and universities frequently use articulate alumni in the admissions recruitment process. Alumni recruiters, especially in areas far from the main campus, help save costly and time-consuming travel by members of the admissions staff. In addition, alumni recruiters are often perceived by prospective students as more credible than paid staff. For these reasons, a few two-year colleges have placed administrative control of alumni programming in the admissions office.

Other relatively new two-year college alumni associations, seeking to cultivate alumni now and ask for money later, see job placement as the most important component of their present alumni program and have placed the alumni relations function within the career development/job placement department. Some schools view alumni relations as an extension of student activities and assign student and alumni programming to the same department. Others identify graduate follow-up as their most important need and place alumni relations within the control of the campus research office. Whatever the campus structure for alumni programming, it is important that it work for that college and meet the needs of its alumni.

Perhaps the most vital aspect of alumni relations at any college or university is the people in the program—alumni volunteers, paid staff, and enrolled students. Volunteers can make or break an alumni program. The entire process of recruiting the proper people, placing them in appropriate assignments, training and motivating them, and evaluating their performance, though it requires significant time, is the key to successful alumni programs. However, the vitally important area of alumni voluntarism is frequently the most neglected, and alumni officers share horror stories about problems experienced because they did not spend enough time on volunteer development.

Whether the aim is establishing a new alumni program, rebuilding an old one, or maintaining a program at its current level, certain elements are common to the volunteer recruitment process. One of the most important is to recruit the right people, which requires an understanding of what the institution wants the alumni program to accomplish. Fund raising, for example, requires certain skills, experience, background, training, and time commitments. Activities such as finding jobs for fellow alumni, lobbying on behalf of the college, serving as role models for current students, planning special events, or advising the college on development of academic programs require others. In fact, further fine-tuning is needed to staff telephones during a "phonathon," meet face-to-face with corporate executives, write letters, or address civic organizations. Each assignment requires different abilities.

We must know how many volunteers are needed and when, whether they are loyal alumni and truly want to help, and whether they have leadership potential. We must be certain that our volunteers will accept all persons, regardless of race, religion, sex, national origin, or political beliefs; can converse easily with others and listen well; and want to be part of a team effort.

Most of these skills and personal qualities can be determined only in a personal interview. The best volunteer programs have leaders who take time to seek strong prospects, conduct personal interviews, and learn firsthand whether the prospects are right for their organization. New recruits need a comprehensive orientation, followed by opportunities for growth and development, as well as responsible, suitable assignments. The individual's preferences, work and life experiences, and educational preparation must be taken into account. Throughout the volunteer assignment the organization must offer challenging work and recognition for achievement. Recognition can take many forms, from a simple "thank you" to plaques, certificates, or dinners. Whatever the form, the concept should never be overlooked.

Effective volunteers will go a long way toward ensuring the success of an alumni program, but staff support and a variety of resources are also essential. When the goals of the alumni association and the college are consistent, the paid staff in the alumni office must provide the necessary backup. This support might be the handling of simple correspondence or more complex tasks such as developing alumni publications, coordinating fund-raising efforts, processing pledges, and scheduling meetings. The job placement department might be called on to provide additional assistance for alumni, and the computer center might be asked to write a program for alumni records.

Too often, community colleges in the early stages of developing alumni programs do not provide this support, and alumni volunteers quickly become frustrated and alienated. Computer support, once a luxury for two-year college alumni groups, is now a necessity. Whereas a decade ago the only alternative to manual record keeping was to use the college mainframe and computer staff, low-cost microcomputers and a wide range of affordable software now put computerized records within the reach of most alumni associations. Computerized records allow quick access to details of alumni interests and vocations, financial information, and accurate mailing lists for a variety of uses. Ease of mail communication is important: just as an effective alumni program is unquestionably the key to successful fund raising, so communication is unquestionably the key to having and keeping effective people in your alumni program. Naylor (1973) and Wilson (1979) provide additional guidance on the management of volunteer programs.

To sum up, then, it is clear that two-year institutions are learning from their four-year counterparts that alumni are a supremely important reservoir on which to draw for dollars and many other benefits. But these rewards are usually the by-products of genuine efforts by colleges to maintain a mutually beneficial affiliation with their alumni.

References

Naylor, H. H. *Volunteers Today: Finding, Training, and Working with Them.* New York: Dryden Associates, 1973.

Rowland, A. W. (ed.). *Handbook of Institutional Advancement: A Modern Guide to Executive Management, Institutional Relations, Fund Raising, Alumni Administration, Government Relations, Publications, Periodicals, and Enrollment Management.* (2nd ed.) San Francisco: Jossey-Bass, 1986.

Wilson, M. *The Effective Management of Volunteer Programs.* Boulder, Colo.: Volunteer Management Associates, 1979.

Richard J. Pokrass is director of college relations and publications at Burlington County College, Pemberton, New Jersey.

Alternative Education/ Alternative Revenue

- A. Contract Training: Public and Private Sector Models
- B. Media Technology Begets Revenue

Contract training not only means additional institutional revenue but is an important business, industry, and public agency connection for the community college.

A.
Contract Training: Public and Private Sector Models

Raymond Lestina, Beverly A. Curry

The comprehensive community college arose chiefly to meet the growing emphasis on higher education placed on educational institutions by the passage of the G.I. Bill of 1944. Returning veterans could increase their earning power and career potential by taking advantage of the educational opportunities provided for them (Blocker, Plummer, and Richardson, 1965). These new entrants to the two-year colleges not only reshaped the college community but brought a host of external affiliations that ultimately became fresh sources of revenue.

The process occurred naturally. To ensure that programs for careers were properly designed (that is, aligned with the needs of business, industry, and external organizations as well as of students), relationships with representatives of the specific occupations were identified. Often these relationships took the form of consultancies and advisory committee memberships. Soon businesses and organizations saw the community college as an economical resource for upgrading the professional skills of staff, as well as a unique access to additional facilities, expertise, and personnel (Powers, Powers, Betz, and Aslanian, 1988). As training opportunities were presented to instructional administrators, many campuses formed separate functional units to handle the training requests.

By the 1970s, community colleges in every region of the country were engaged in full-fledged quests for training contracts with business, manufacturers, health care providers, government agencies, and a host of other profit and nonprofit enterprises. Few colleges, however, did more than cover expenses. In fact, the real revenue source in many cases was the state, since those trained were often folded into the college's overall full-time equivalent student report to state agencies.

In the early 1980s, tuition and state revenues began to decline, and community colleges turned to partnerships with businesses and agencies to increase revenues. The Employee Development Institute (EDI), Triton College's major provider of training for business and industry, is an excellent example of effective contract training for revenue enhancement. Training activity at Triton is allied with the regional economic development center, Mid-Metro Regional Development, Incorporated. Mid-Metro offers such services to the local community as advice on small business development; export, trade and government procurement; business retention; new ventures incubation; and convention and tourism development. Triton College's president chairs the community-based board of directors.

Between 1985 and 1988, Triton's EDI, with a professional account staff of five, averaged two hundred on-site contracts, fifty-five seminars, and eighty short-term training programs per year. Ninety percent of contract training programs at Triton are noncredit and 10 percent are degree-credit courses. Approximately 85 percent of the contract training programs are offered at the business location, 15 percent on campus. The majority are tailored to the specific needs of an organization. Customized content is a selling point emphasized in all advertising copy.

Even with significant expansion in service contracts and revenues, competition in contract training has increased substantially over the past five years. The primary competitors include private consulting firms, proprietary schools, four-year colleges and universities, formatted self-teaching videos, professional associations, and vendor-supplied training. An aggressive marketing strategy is clearly vital to a community college's success in the contract training area.

For EDI, effective marketing begins with research. First, information about the types of businesses and organizations in the service delivery area is developed. Data are accumulated on the "typed" product or service (manufacturing, retail, banking, and so on), number and classification of employees, scope of market, and geographic location. All the information is needed to segment the various markets and then identify the training needs of each market segment. A marketing plan based on the research outlines promotional strategies. These include direct mail (brochures), media advertising, personalized letter with follow-up telephone call (only feasible in low volume), personal-contact networking through business and professional associations, and cold calls by the professional staff or Triton's president to the company chief executive officer, with follow-up by the EDI staff. This last strategy is very powerful. Rarely does an industry's chief executive officer turn down a request from a college president for an appointment. Once a meeting has taken place, the process accelerates: the company representatives are more responsive when their chief executive officer has been involved.

A vital component in marketing strategy is the development of repeat business, without which it is difficult if not impossible to generate profit consistently. At Triton College, 50 to 60 percent of a year's contract training business is with organizations that have previously contracted with the college. The keys to this success are quick response, flexibility in adjusting the training program content, solving problems as they arise, and, most important, delivering high-quality training. Satisfied clients are one of the most effective marketing tools available: they will repeatedly purchase additional contract training from the college, inform their peers in other organizations of the quality of training, and write testimonials that can be used as copy in other marketing materials.

Triton's EDI consists essentially of a mid-management-level group of account executives whose role is to solicit training contracts from business and industry, manage the development, monitor the implementation of the contract training program, and serve as liaison between the company and the college. Once a specific lead is generated, the college account executive needs to follow a number of steps to turn a contact into a contract.

The creative revenue-producing partnerships that have evolved at Triton College resulted from this type of cooperation and follow three significant models: the contract or "workplace" model, the cosponsorship/coprovidership model, and the distance learning model.

Contract or "Workplace" Model

The traditional "workplace," or contract, model is the most common. When a business or organization has a specific educational need, contracts for training, whether the program is new or already developed, are designed to meet the needs of that particular group. In all such requests companies guarantee the enrollment. Programs are sited for the convenience of the audience. Contracting for training with the local community college is considerably less expensive than using an outside consultant who might charge $200 to $300 per person for a group of thirty to forty. Besides serving industry and the community, contracting generates revenue for the college.

The specific steps of the contract model are as follows:

1. Meeting with the appropriate company representative to clarify the nature of the training need and gather additional information about the potential training topics.

2. Identification of subject matter experts and possible instructors.

3. Meeting with the company representative, subject matter expert or instructor, and college account executive. During this meeting, additional information concerning the training program will be discussed (for example, who will be trained, assessments, refinement of content). In addition, the company representative will have the opportunity to interview the potential instructor.

4. Development of the training proposal. The college executive will write a proposal that includes an outline of the training program content, dates and times, costs, and method of billing. The proposal should be concise.

5. Presentation of proposal. The account executive and company representative meet to discuss the terms of the proposal and determine whether any revisions are necessary. At this point the proposal will either be accepted, rejected, put on hold, or returned for revisions. Revisions usually pertain to program content, length of program, or start date.

6. Acceptance of the training proposal. Once the proposal is accepted and contract signed by the company representative, the instructor is hired by the college and begins the implementation of the program.

7. Orientation and assessment. During this step the instructor does the following:
- Learns the company's procedures, policies, and products, and becomes familiar with the facility
- Meets with appropriate company personnel (for example, supervisors, foremen, employees, personnel director)
- Conducts assessments as agreed in the proposal
- Prepares training materials and handouts
- Advises account executive if textbooks need to be ordered.

The account executive does the following:
- Arranges for a classroom or lab if training is to be conducted on campus
- Orders textbooks
- Coordinates all administrative details.

8. Provision of training. It is important that the account executive maintain communication with the instructor and the company representative, so that he or she can work through any problems that arise.

9. Evaluation. All employees participating in the training program are asked to complete a written evaluation of both course and instructor. Summaries of all evaluations are sent to the company representative and instructor. The account executive and instructor also meet with the company representative to evaluate the program verbally.

10. Follow-up. Company is billed. Account executive contacts company representative to discuss future contract training programs.

Cosponsorships Model

In addition to the EDI, already discussed, another highly effective contract training arm at Triton College is the Continuing Education Center for Health Professionals (CECHP). For the past fourteen years Triton's CECHP has developed high-quality educational programs, on the cosponsorship/coprovidership model, that have a positive effect on the professional growth of over 10,000 health care practitioners annually. A staff of health professionals with master's degrees respond quickly, creatively, and effectively to the needs of health professionals for continuing education in-service training.

The CECHP voluntarily sought and received institutional accreditation for continuing education from seven national professional organizations, the Illinois Department of Professional Regulation, and the Illinois Department of Public Health. For example, CECHP staff are approved as providers of continuing education for nurses by the American Nurses' Association.

Although competition has increased in the last five years, Triton's CECHP has continued to grow in enrollment and revenue because of its commitment to quality control, the certification capability of external accreditations, and, not least, the development of marketing strategies, especially on the cosponsorship/coprovidership model.

When a program is opened up to include other business organizations or individuals to defray costs, the cosponsorship model emerges. Cosponsorship is a means whereby another agency or group of interested professionals (associations, for example) joins a community college to provide a planned learning experience. The cosponsoring agency is listed as such in the promotional literature. The responsibilities and involvement of each cosponsoring agency are determined by mutual agreement. In this model, a number of employees from the cosponsoring agency might attend an event without financial charge to the agency. Partners might agree to an equal distribution of excess revenues after all bills are paid. These agreements should produce win/win situations for both parties.

In this model, which is easily adapted to working with an agency, professional organization, college, or university, initial contact is made either by agency or the CECHP representative identifying an educational need. Planning and implementation of this type of nursing continuing education takes at least six months.

Most CECHP activities cosponsored with the Triton College credit area have a core committee for the purpose of administering and coordinating the event. Comprising representatives from each of the agency nursing divisions, including education, the vice-president of patient care services, and the Triton College coordinator of continuing education for nursing, the core committee is ultimately accountable for the high quality and educational soundness of the total program. To meet these responsibilities, the chairperson of the core committee, the Triton College CECHP, the coordinator of nursing continuing education, and the core committee members have final review and determine the appropriateness and quality of the continuing education program.

Each cosponsored offering is first planned by a subcomponent of the core committee, a task force composed usually of two to five individuals with particular expertise in the content area of the offering. This group establishes the objectives and content, ensures accuracy and currency, and "certifies" the competency of the instructors and handouts.

Step 1: Generation of the Broad Concept. Ideas for viable nursing continuing education offerings come from many sources: administrators or staff nurses may have areas of expertise to share or may have specific needs they know their peers have also; the core committee for the nursing continuing education program may make specific suggestions; and registrants at all nursing continuing education offerings are given the opportunity to suggest future topics. In all instances, the first step is a discussion of the idea with the director of the nursing division.

The task force next meets to discuss:
- General program objectives: what the program is supposed to accomplish
- Possible target audience: level of knowledge, size, and the college's ability to tap
- Appropriateness of the topic to the audience
- General competition: how many other similar programs are being offered in the area
- Best teaching methodologies or format and the importance of using adult education principles, particularly regarding relevance of topic and involvement of registrants, are stressed
- Selection of faculty: a preferred and a possible backup slate should be chosen
- Potential dates: consideration of information about upcoming or standing conferences (regional or national) in the specialty area
- Best location: at hospital, Triton, or elsewhere.

Step 2: Information Gathering. During this phase, the task force should do the following:
- Check possible dates for conflict with other major continuing education providers in the area (this does not guarantee lack of conflict, but lessens the chance of major problems)
- Check location and food service facilities, if applicable
- Refine program ideas, objectives, and projected format; then discuss as widely as possible with potential registrants to assess their opinions, interest, and perceived need
- Make preliminary contact with desired faculty by phone or letter.

Step 3: Decision. The task force now considers the information gathered in stage 2 and makes the critical decision whether to present the program offering.

If they proceed, the following activities must be accomplished:
- Mutually agreed contract written by CECHP staff and signed by a Triton administrator and cosponsoring agency outlining financial arrangements, responsibilities, and so on
- Objectives, format, and schedule finalized
- Definite date selected
- Final faculty or speaker decisions signed
- Final location chosen
- Methods and tools evaluated as determined by American Nurses' Association (ANA) approved criteria
- Task list and assignments completed—in writing
- Marketing plans discussed
- Continuing education offering submitted for peer review according to Triton College-approved ANA criteria.

Step 4: Confirmation. At this stage all program arrangements and details are confirmed, usually in writing; speakers or faculty are confirmed in writing; and the brochure is developed (the printer's draft should be approved by the core committee).

Step 5: Preprogram Stage. Approximately three to four weeks before the program date, a series of checks and reconfirmation procedures are implemented:
- Reminder-reconfirmation letters sent out to faculty
- Moderator duties assigned
- Progress communication from CECHP chairperson of task force (for example, current registration)
- Final recap of all plans.

Step 6: The Program Itself. The day of the program can be almost anticlimactic; all the planning is completed and details should be accomplished. Task force members serve mainly as the hospitality group, meeting registrants, attending to faculty, and generally mixing to serve as resource persons. Evaluations are collected at the end of the day in exchange for the continuing education certificates.

Step 7: Wrap-Up Period. After the program offering, the following should be accomplished:
- Evaluations summarized by CECHP and sent out to speakers by the task force with thank-you letters, honorariums included
- Survey of files in the CECHP office: copies of all correspondence, attendance lists, certificates awarded, program objectives, faculty vitae, handouts, and copies of minutes of all planning meetings
- Evaluation meeting with the core committee to discuss what happened and future plans or modifications for additional programming.

Using the wrap-up period to identify needs for additional programming sets the wheels into motion for an additional marketing strategy, the development of a "tracking model." Continuing education for health professionals consists of learning activities intended to build on the education and experience of professional training, to enhance practice, education, administration, research, or theory development and improve an individual's ability to deal with the health of the public. A tracking model allows the health professional to build his or her knowledge and practice skills. By identifying in a carefully sequenced program the skills necessary for developing or enhancing a clinical specialty, the tracking model provides individuals and employers a carefully planned opportunity to meet the needs of nursing practice.

Colleges and agencies have cooperated for years to serve the interests of both. As collaborators they move from individual goals and solve problems through the convergence of values and by addressing the needs of the audience to be served. Needs are met even beyond the interests of the individual parties in the relationship.

References

Blocker, C. E., Plummer, R. H., and Richardson, R. C., Jr. *The Two-Year College: A Social Synthesis.* Englewood Cliffs, N.J.: Prentice-Hall, 1965.

Powers, D. R., Powers, M. F., Betz, F., and Aslanian, C. B. *Higher Education in Partnerships with Industry: Opportunities and Strategies for Training, Research, and Economic Development.* San Francisco: Jossey-Bass, 1988.

Raymond Lestina is associate dean for continuing education and director of the Employee Development Institute at Triton College, River Grove, Illinois.

Beverly A. Curry is associate dean for the Continuing Education Center for Health Professionals at Triton College, having moved to that position from the nursing faculty.

Media delivery systems such as teleconferencing, Instructional Television Fixed Service, and cable networks are examined for their revenue-enhancing potential.

B. Media Technology Begets Revenue

Jana B. Kooi

Ever since RCA's idea of broadcasting pictures long distances became a reality in New York in 1936, the public has been fascinated by this electronic miracle. Attempts at providing education through various broadcast systems have been made often during the last fifty years, but with minimal success, largely because traditional classroom instruction does not translate well without student interaction or variety of action in presentation.

Distance learning is, nonetheless, an alternative means of meeting the educational delivery needs in a community college district and at the same time of expanding into satellite communities outside the district, even nationally. It allows instruction to be offered in nontraditional time slots and serves a target population that may not otherwise enroll in any college program. Financially, the educational products developed or purchased generally pay for themselves.

The distance learning model, as a revenue-generating enterprise developed at Triton College, focuses on traditional and nontraditional learning experiences delivered in a highly functional although nontraditional manner. The several areas of distance learning at Triton (cable network, Instructional Television Fixed Service, and satellite video teleconferencing) function in an essentially integrated way so the direction taken best represents the needs and philosophy of the institution.

Cable Network

The mere mention of "educational cable television" can bring on yawns and immediate channel flipping, but the right combination of produced and purchased shows, professional and creative talent, and sponsored or supported programming can provide an exciting alternative educational vehicle. In fact, among Triton's continuing education offerings, this area has the greatest potential for revenue gain, and an equal risk of loss. In large part, the potential for loss arises from the significant up-front investment in staff and equipment to support the programming, all before any profits come in.

The technical capabilities of a cable television system can range from simple to sophisticated, depending on the initial and long-term investments the college is willing to make. It may choose a system that is essentially playback, with no in-house production facilities or staff. The programming format in this system comprises telecourses or other programs that are purchased because they are in line with the programming philosophy of the institution. In addition to equipment, costs include minimal playback staff, purchase of telecourses and shows, equipment maintenance, licensing fees, marketing of telecourses, and costs of instructors to flesh out the telecourses. This is a very cost-effective method. After the initial purchase of equipment, the yearly revenue of telecourses outweighs the yearly costs.

Although this system should consistently provide a modest yearly income, it does have drawbacks. The network cannot be used effectively for public relations for the institution. Promotions of the network have to be purchased outside, which is costly, and the integration of the promotions into other programming often looks amateurish. The overall effect is pleasant to the public (again, depending on the quality of purchased programming) but smacks of "educational television."

Any system more sophisticated than this requires a major financial commitment of equipment and staff for a combination of playback and in-house production. Of course, the addition of a production studio opens up the college's promotional possibilities for academic-based entertainment programming and outside production contracts. The development and management of these components can make this system a financial drain or a major revenue source for the institution.

The real potential for revenue comes from video productions sponsored by contracts with business and industry. At Triton College a unique partnership has occurred. The Employee Development Institute (EDI) that procures contract training for business and industry also sells the network sponsorships and video production capabilities of the television station.

Instructional Television Fixed Service

The second area of distance learning is Instructional Television Fixed Service (ITFS), a broadcast license issued by the Federal Communications Commission to educational organizations for the transmission of instructional, cultural, and other types of educational material to one or more fixed receiving locations. The open-air signal is transmitted via microwave at a frequency of 2500-2700 MegaHertz.

The primary and most productive use of ITFS is custom-designed interactive video conferencing. An excellent example is the Emergency Medical Technician (EMT) training for firefighters developed by the Continuing Education Center for Health Professionals (CECHP) at Triton College. Since all firefighters are required to go through periodic retraining in EMT, a custom-designed program was developed that could be aired to multiple fire stations during firefighters' work hours. The taped training program was produced by Triton's television studio, scripted by Triton's CECHP department, and hosted by one of Triton's allied health faculty. The taped shows were aired several times a week with a live wraparound segment hosted by the allied health faculty. The firefighters call in questions during the live part of the show, speaking directly to the instructor and professional guests, who answer the questions on air. There is an initial cost for production of the taped series, but once production is completed the only cost is the instructor, who can be used in a ratio to students of one to hundreds. This model of distance learning functions most effectively and efficiently with an in-house production studio and staff. There is also a second option: the institution can function solely as receive and transmission sites. This option necessarily involves an agreement with other institutions or production studios to produce the taped program and the wraparound program to be transmitted to and received by the institution, and in turn transmitted to receiver sites in the college district or receive area.

Satellite Video Teleconferencing

The satellite video teleconferencing area is divided into two parts: (1) receive teleconferences and (2) produced teleconferences. A receive teleconference is a packaged, presold, live program that is purchased for a minimal cost, marketed to a targeted audience and presented, via satellite, live at the institution. If the following steps are taken, this can be a strong revenue-generating endeavor:

1. When purchasing a teleconference, carefully check the quality and

content of the production. Ask to see video clips of previous programs the company or institution has produced. Many of the current teleconferences available are of mediocre quality. Even though your institution did not produce the program, its name is the one the audience will associate with the poor production.

The content of a teleconference is not always as advertised. In a production company's desire to make their products more salable, they may elaborate the topic and content of the teleconference to include a larger target audience. Ask the company specific questions about subject matter and presenters. The extra effort will be well spent.

2. When marketing a teleconference, it is preferable to involve a cosponsoring agency or organization. This involvement will provide a built-in audience and more support for a marketing effort.

3. This next step is optional but can increase the quality of the event for the audience. A live wraparound before or after the satellite production on the same or expanded topic areas gives the audience a sense of having it brought home to their needs and allows them to increase their field of knowledge by deeper discussion than the usual one- or two-hour teleconference provides. The wraparound and the received teleconference can also be sent to other receiver sites via ITFS, if more space is needed, or can be taped and shown at other times.

There is another important issue, a financial one, in the decision to produce and distribute video teleconferences. The initial cost of uplink capability or rental is the only one the institution *must* absorb; there need be no future cost, because grants, sponsorships, and corporate training contracts can ease the burden and actually provide substantial revenue if the college is successful in procuring endorsements. Just as with the cable network, the institution must find cosponsoring groups: it would be less than prudent to produce a teleconference without a cosponsor and a guaranteed target audience. The competition from commercial teleconference distributors is too great to produce teleconferencing merely with the hope that it will sell. There are other points to remember to ensure a successful teleconference: (1) Video teleconferencing does not sell itself. There should be a private audience designated to receive the production, such as a training session for corporation managers. Also, it is important in marketing the teleconference not only to mail information but to establish personal contacts within each reception site. This is the best way to procure business and guarantee return business. (2) Once the teleconference has been sold to a reception site, very specific written communications must take place with the designated site coordinator. Many problems occur when a coordinator does not understand the procedures and communications systems.

In summary, then, video teleconferencing, ITFS, and cable network are all available as means for the community college not only to serve the educational needs of its community in the broadest geographical way but also to enhance its revenues. Like commercial TV, however, educational TV is a risky business. Because the viewing public is used to the glitz and professionalism of commercial television, unless an institution is willing to commit to high standards in technical productions, on-air talent, professional staff, and marketing efforts, distance learning as a significant revenue resource is not a viable option. If the challenges are met, however, distance learning can be one of the most exciting and profitable endeavors an institution can make.

Jana B. Kooi is associate vice-president for external academic affairs at Triton College, River Grove, Illinois.

Economic development is tied in most states to the community college's role in training and retraining of employees to meet industry needs.

Economic Development, the Community College, and Technology Training

Steve Maradian

Economic Reality

Two-year colleges are often appealed to for economic development services ranging from basic literacy programs to high technology training in areas such as computer-assisted design (CAD), computer-integrated manufacturing (CIM), and statistic process control (SPC). This recent and important trend among community colleges fine-tunes economic development activities to very specific needs of local communities and the state. State and local government agencies are increasingly interested in joint economic development efforts with two-year colleges, particularly when the linkage results in the creation of more jobs and improves the quality of life for the communities served.

Two-year colleges are called on because they are best prepared to provide a full range of services that access technology. They ensure that local industry possesses the technological know-how to develop the products and services to improve their production and service capabilities, by training employees in the use of those new technologies. Those economic development training programs have been funded in many ways, including state subsidy, local tax levies, and direct fees. Training services have made an important contribution to economic recovery, but their potential for expansion in response to the training needs of business and industry is important at a time when state, federal, and local resources are hard pressed to support the new initiatives required by a technological society.

The critical issue is funding. "There are, certainly, strains and questions arising from the growing collaboration. Community colleges' expanding ties with business and labor are requiring adjustments in procedures and financing, such as putting together packages of training funds from several government programs" (Fields, 1988, p. 30). This issue must be addressed constructively, recognizing the limits of public resources.

In the long term, the most important action in which community and technical colleges must become involved is the development of public policy. There must be, in the true sense, public funding of education. That remains the best hope for sustaining the level of activity expected of the two-year college. James McKenney, associate director of the Keeping America Working Project at the American Association of Community and Junior Colleges notes: "No state . . . has flatly rejected the idea of using tax funds to help pay for some of the instruction needed by industry, and I don't know of any state where there has been a big public debate over such use of tax funds" (Fields, 1988, p. 33). College presidents must become active at the local, state, and national levels to shape funding policies that provide the resources for these very necessary services.

For the short term, given the reality of funding limitations, community college leaders have already begun to cultivate alternative funding sources aggressively. New sources must be found if they are to continue to provide the level and range of educational and economic development activities their service districts expect. How they are found is frequently a reflection of the institution's creativity, resourcefulness, and aggressiveness.

Ambiguity of Definition

It is also important to consider what is meant by the term *alternative funding*. Specifically, any source with potential that has not previously been tapped might be considered alternative. In this way, what is standard in one district or state may not be so considered in another. In Massachusetts, for example, funding for educational programs offered in the evening, off campus, or on weekends, for credit or noncredit, is excluded from public funding. Such programs are required to be self-supporting. The prohibition against using state resources for these activities limits the institution's capacity to respond to the needs of business and industry. Thus, in Massachusetts, funding for such programs might be considered alternative. Conversely, the state of Florida supports most instructional programs regardless of when the course is offered or what its structure. The definition of alternative shifts from state to state, sometimes even from locale to locale.

In Ohio, business and industry training and retraining are major initiatives articulated by the board of regents, the chancellor, and the governor. Nevertheless, and even though public subsidy to support these efforts is virtually nonexistent, the two-year colleges in Ohio have been significantly instrumental in the state's recent economic turnaround. Industry is seeking well-trained technicians in particular, and the two-year college is a ready source of such talent. Without state subsidy, Ohio administrators have become adept at tapping nontraditional funding resources to support these activities.

Belmont Technical College, in southeastern Ohio, is located in an area once dominated by steel, coal, and glass manufacturing. The college has helped rebuild a community devastated by high unemployment due to the migration of industry, plant closings, and strained labor-management relations. Concentrated efforts have been directed at all aspects of economic development, including the formation of an incubation center in concert with the county development agency, worker training and retraining programs, consulting services to industries, technology transfer, and redevelopment and restoration efforts of abandoned structures as part of the college's new mission.

Faced with the opportunity to expand its educational program in mining technology, along with a desire to redevelop abandoned land, the college sought and received funds from the state department of natural resources and local township trustees to reclaim land abandoned by former coal-mining companies. The college was able to support the reclamation costs involved in transforming twenty acres of unusable land into a community recreational area.

In terms of educational value, the reclamation project served as a learning laboratory for students in the mining program. The funds generated from the project supplemented and enhanced the state subsidy provided by full-time equivalent student enrollments. An added benefit, unanticipated by the college, was the discovery within the reclamation area of coal valued at approximately $310,000 (preextraction value), which was sold at a profit of $75,000.

Throughout the five-year life of this project, approximately $500,000 was generated from "nontraditional" sources. In addition, the effort provided valuable educational opportunities for students and served to promote important economic and community development activities. One additional benefit realized by the college has been the annual contributing of "gifts" from local mining companies and professional coal-mining associations.

The college's reclamation efforts were so successful that they have expanded into the area of preservation and restoration of historically significant buildings. For that project, the college solicited financial support from the National Trust for Historic Preservation to develop a "preservation and restoration" technology degree program. Federal Economic Development Administration funds were also sought and will be used to "leverage" state instructional subsidies. Although the college did not anticipate entering real estate development as a business, the program serves many purposes: it spurs economic development, rebuilds the community, safeguards cultural aspects of the community, and prepares students for exciting career opportunities.

Edison State Community College, in central Ohio, also used college property to generate revenues, but in a very different way from Belmont Technical College. Edison took advantage of the fact that tracts of college land were not in use, capitalized on the opportunity, and rented vacant property to local farmers. Although the income is not significant in terms of total budget dollars, it demonstrates that two-year colleges are truly expansive in their search for nontraditional funding.

One important outcome of economic development is improvement of the quality of life of the community. Two-year colleges promote quality of life by nurturing a skilled work force, turning despair in communities to hope and prosperity. Numerous Ohio colleges have been successful in attracting state department of development support for skill upgrading of the existing industrial work force. One example of a successful linkage is the college's contracting with a local steel manufacturing company to upgrade the skills of its work force. Funded again by state agencies, Belmont Technical College was able to develop a training operation for some hundred employees in "high-tech" manufacturing processes. The project is similar to entrepreneurial efforts in community colleges across the country and illustrates the community college's capabilities in these areas.

The training effort expanded Belmont's economic development efforts in the upgrading of skills and established a three-way partnership agreement with the United Steelworkers of America, the college, and the steel manufacturing company. Without this alternative support, the school would have found it very difficult to fund the program. Instructional subsidies would simply have been inadequate. "Leveraging" of dollars—matching one agency's funding with subsidy dollars—along with income from student fees put the venture on a sound footing. In addition, the basis for a long-term relationship with a major manufacturer and a union has been developed, so that the next joint project may be easier.

Much attention has been directed in the literature to business-industry partnerships that link community colleges with larger industries. Journal articles highlight success stories such as Tyler Junior College's program to save 1,400 Goodyear Tire manufacturing jobs, Delta College's training center at General Motors, Ohio's Thomas Edison programs, Sinclair Community College's programs with General Motors, the Keeping America Working Project partnership, and the College of Lake County's programs with the U.S. Department of Defense.

Belmont Technical College's efforts with workers recently displaced by plant shutdowns combined the college with local industry representatives and officials of the United Steelworkers' union, representing some 240 workers who had lost their jobs. The college staff called together state economic assistance teams representing the Job Training Partnership Act (JTPA), union officials, plant owners, and public officials to develop a dislocated workers training program.

As a result of aggressive action, the college was included in the shutdown agreement between the union and company owners, which included $750 in educational assistance for each eligible dislocated worker. The college, with union support, leveraged JTPA Title III dollars, industry dollars, and state subsidy to provide a comprehensive assessment and training program for workers who lacked the skills to compete in a work force. The funds combined to provide some $3,300 per person for training available over eighteen months. In this way, nontraditional dollars targeted to specialized needs supported the primary purpose of a two-year college and at the same time expanded the use of those dollars for other college services.

Another Belmont College enterprise shows how external funding can be used to meet institutional and student needs. As in other rural community or technical colleges, Belmont students face many barriers to educational success. Child-care services are high on the list. The college sought funds to expand its day-care services and to provide "night care" services as well. Working with local welfare department officials, the college gained eligibility for approximately 90 percent of the families utilizing day-care services. The welfare department thus "subsidizes" the cost of day-care services. Not only has the barrier been removed, but the additional dollars are used by the college to enhance business and industry programs.

The college further identified a need for day care among evening students who are also confronted by this barrier to access. Through a State Department of Education grant (normally directed to secondary schools), a unique "Nightwatch" program was made available to students. An added benefit is increased enrollments during evening hours, with corresponding increased instructional subsidies that can be directed to nonrevenue activities in the business and industry services division.

What can be seen from this discussion is that community and technical colleges, both large or small, are essential to economic development, regardless of the size of the community or whether it is rural, urban, or suburban. The interim question of who pays the bills remains a campus-based one. Cultivating local resources, seeking private dollars, developing and acquiring funds available through state, federal, and local resources (that historically have not been directed to higher education) are part of the answer. In the meantime, community college leaders must not relax and wait for public policy to catch up with the demands. They must seek nontraditional funding opportunities to sustain economic development activities begun throughout the last decade, demonstrating again the importance of two-year colleges in American life.

Reference

Fields, C. "Community Colleges Discover They Are at the Right Place at the Right Time." *Governing*, February 1988, pp. 30-35.

Steve Maradian is president of Belmont Technical College, St. Clairsville, Ohio.

Adaptation, Darwin's concept for survival, is precisely what this chapter suggests: nonprofit community college undertaking for-profit ventures.

Entrepreneurship in the Community College: Revenue Diversification

Richard W. Brightman

Then and Now

The heyday of community colleges in the 1960s and early 1970s, marked by almost unlimited resources for expansion, will not return. This is not to say that the need to serve more students with a greater variety of courses has been fully met. To the contrary, a larger percentage of high school graduates now goes to college than twenty years ago (61 percent versus 40 percent), and the number of older students is also increasing (34 percent of all college students are over twenty-five [Friedrich, 1982]).

The Carnegie Council on Policy Issues in Higher Education (1980) lists community colleges as the least vulnerable to enrollment declines among institutions of higher education because "they enjoy strong support and appeal to . . . enlarging categories of students: minorities . . . adults, and part-time students" (p. 58). Community colleges continue to add to their functions, particularly in nonvocational and nonacademic areas. The predicament, then, is not reduced public interest in collegiate education but rather reduced finances.

The first response of two-year colleges to the financial crisis has been one of resistance. In the early 1980s in California, for example, heavy lobbying and desperate press conferences, in an effort to sustain programs, were routine. Maintenance was postponed, personnel laid off, expenditures for supplies and equipment reduced, and reserves spent, all with the hope that improved economic circumstances and contrite lawmakers would reverse the situation.

The dire predictions for community colleges have continued. Enrollment of traditional full-time college-age students is down, and demographic studies predict that the size of the traditional college-age group (eighteen to twenty-four) will have fallen about 25 percent by the turn of the century (Carnegie Council on Policy Issues in Higher Education, 1980). Colleges now concede that both public and private support for higher education will likely decline in the years ahead as well.

Although some of the funding reductions have been offset by more efficient operations, the preponderant practice now is retrenchment, cutting back or eliminating programs to balance distressed budgets. A study conducted by the Southern Regional Education Board of twenty retrenching colleges observed this pattern (Mingle, 1981, p. 52):

> A drop in freshman enrollments leads to expenditure cuts, resulting in physical deterioration of the campus, cuts in counseling and in student services, personnel cuts, and sagging morale among faculty who remain. The attitudes of students also are affected as they witness the conflict and deterioration of services. (In some institutions, faculty and staff had directly enlisted students as political allies in fighting staff reductions.) The results were declines in retention rates and, thus, another round of retrenchment.

It is clear that reduced budgets have a dispiriting effect on community college faculty and students. In the past, we may have taken perverse satisfaction in turning away students because we have been full to capacity. Now we fear that even though we admit them, they may turn away from shabby surroundings and run-down equipment.

Coming to Terms with the Situation

There is little point in waiting for government to shore up finances. The federal administration is striving to shift responsibilities from the federal government to state, local, and private agencies and has succeeded in reducing almost every federal student support activity. Social security benefits for dependent children have been phased out. Pell grants have been reduced. Supplemental Educational Opportunity

Grants have been cut. These reductions represent more than half of all federal outlays for higher education. Besides that, community colleges' participation in federal support for students has never been strong: in 1979, a typical year, two-year colleges received only 18 percent of all federal spending for higher education. That was also only 7.4 percent of all sources of community college revenues in 1979 (Breneman and Nelson, 1981).

Contrary to federal policy, there is no reason to believe that state governments will be able to pick up the tab. State government expenditures for higher education may appear to have increased steadily over the years, but when adjusted for inflation, these appropriations have actually decreased.

At the same time that there have been concerns over declining enrollments and financial support, there have also been concerns for maintaining the quality of higher education. Mingle (1981, p. 7), in *Challenges of Retrenchment*, summarizes these as follows:

- Fears that increased competition for students results in "body counting" and "survival of the slickest"
- A need for a code of "fair practices" and for a strengthening of the accreditation process
- The weakening of academic standards and of rigor in such programs as teacher education and the decline in general of meritocratic values in higher education
- The decline in faculty compensation relative to that of other professionals.

Here is the predicament. We must maintain the quality of our programs and even improve it; we must open our doors to increasing numbers who seek our services; and we must do so with reduced public financial support.

Resistance as a viable policy has failed. Another alternative, to cut programs, has already been tried, for example, in California in the mid 1980s, after the legislature expressed an unwillingness to continue financing vocational, recreational, and self-help courses. The next way to adapt is to search for new funding sources.

Coping with the predicament in any systematic way requires a comprehensive approach to developing new sources of revenue for community colleges. One component of that approach is for colleges to go into business. Community colleges have enormous resources, which have traditionally been used almost exclusively for their publicly supported educational and community service programs and otherwise be idle. These resources can earn revenues to support nonprofit activities. For-profit ventures can be thought of as revenue diversification.

Efforts to Widen Sources of Income

Diversification of revenue sources has been practiced by commercial and industrial enterprises for centuries. It serves the purpose of reducing the risk to the organization of relying on one source for all or most of its income. Thus business organizations engage in both vertical and horizontal integration and expand into totally unrelated business ventures. It was not surprising to read that Philip Morris bought the Mission Viejo Company, a real estate development firm, or that F. W. Woolworth, a dime store chain, also operates shoe stores and men's clothing outlets. Should we then be surprised at the notion that public community colleges use their assets, otherwise idle, to go into business?

Revenue diversification after all is not new to higher education. Specific examples are easy to locate: Stanford earns millions of dollars per year from its industrial park in Palo Alto; Skidmore College in New York manufactures heating fuel from drain oil, saving hundreds of thousands per year; the University of Wisconsin has operated a shopping center and office facility for twenty-five years; Emory-Riddle Aeronautical University repairs and rebuilds small aircraft and operates a travel agency; Grinnell College bought a commercial television station, managed it well by hiring professional broadcasters, and sold it five years later for a substantial profit (Barton, Stevens, and Massarsky, Ltd., 1982).

In recent years, a variety of nonprofit organizations have turned to profit-making ventures to provide revenues to support their programs. The Denver Children's Museum earns over 90 percent of its annual budget through money-making ventures; the Metropolitan Museum of Art in New York grosses well over $25 million a year by selling art reproductions; the Delancey Street Foundation, a halfway house for ex-addicts, ex-convicts, and ex-prostitutes, operates a restaurant on Union Street in San Francisco; and Baltimore's Southeast Community Organization profits from a lease-back arrangement with retail stores (Williams, 1982b).

The growth of entrepreneurial spirit in nonprofit organizations is a response to reduced public support for social services and the failure of private philanthropy to fill the void. For-profit ventures are risky and are not automatically successful, but, if investigated with care and with a willingness to hire business and financial expertise, they surely hold no less promise for community colleges than for other nonprofit organizations.

For the purposes of community colleges, a diversification activity is defined as a business venture, either developed or acquired, for which the community college or college district is responsible as a result of its ownership for all or a controlling share of the venture. The purpose of the activity is to make a profit that can be used to help support educational and other related activities.

Being Forewarned

For-profit activities can be operated by any nonprofit institution. But before involving themselves in these activities, the college board of trustees and high-level administrators need to come to terms with frequent accusations directed at for-profit ventures:

"It Must Be Illegal." Although no investigation has suggested that it is illegal for community colleges, as nonprofit institutions, to earn money, the allegation is made. Colleges are commonly an arm of the state and are more usually considered to be fund-spending than fund-earning institutions. Nevertheless, colleges do earn funds, and in a number of ways. The Internal Revenue Service encourages nonprofit organizations to engage in profit-making ventures (Hopkins, 1982).

"The State Will Take the Money Away." This is a political comment rather than an economic one. In most states the level of support for the community colleges has been equally a political question. States will usually ignore any community college's alternative sources of revenue.

"It Competes with Local Business." This comment reflects concern that community support for the college will be lost if the college enters the marketplace in competition with local enterprise. A strong argument can be mounted that the local community will benefit from the college's increasing independence from tax revenues.

"It Diverts Resources from the Primary Function of the College." This will be true if it is permitted. To be successful at both nonprofit educational purposes and for-profit ventures, colleges must ensure that there is a clear distinction between them in the allocation of our resources. Just as it is a mistake to appoint a development officer on a part-time basis and expect fund-raising success, it is a mistake to expect a harried dean to start a business venture in his or her spare time. Success with this idea will take the full attention of those who are not involved with other affairs of the college.

"Who Gets the Profits?" The answer to this question must be determined through the regular budget process. If the program is related to food service, for example, the food service faculty are granted the proceeds to maintain and improve their program. If the operation becomes extraordinarily profitable, they should expect the profits to be used to support other programs as well.

"It's Contrary to Our Ideals." Educating our youth and other members of our community is such a valuable social service that the public should be more than willing to support it with taxes. Nevertheless, tax revenues are declining. Nonprofit institutions that have been reluctant to enter profit-seeking operations are having a change of heart. "The old attitude of 'we won't dirty our hands like that' is breaking down," according to an official of the Rockefeller Brothers Fund. "A lot of people are

realizing that constant fund raising, and sometimes begging, aren't much fun either" (Williams, 1982a).

Two Types of For-Profit Activities

The reality is that community colleges across the country are already into business ventures. In discussing these, it is important to distinguish between two types of for-profit activities: those that are related to the nonprofit purposes of the colleges and those that are not. If the for-profit activities are unrelated to the nonprofit purposes, the profits are taxable, according to the Internal Revenue Service (IRS). For example, if a college leases space in a local shopping center and starts a video arcade, the profits from this venture are taxable unless there is a substantive relationship between operating an arcade and the nonprofit purposes of the college. One must pay attention to the tax-exempt status that the college enjoys as a nonprofit institution. Whether or not that status is jeopardized by for-profit ventures depends on how the ventures are organized and the amount of revenue generated.

The literature suggests that as long as the profit-making activities are organized separately, that is, are separate corporations with no overlapping directorates, and as long as the revenue from for-profit ventures does not exceed 35 percent of the college's total income, there is no danger that the IRS will revoke the college's tax-exempt status. Moreover, the degree to which the nonprofit organization participates in equity ownership of the for-profit corporation should not exceed 80 percent (Williams, 1982a).

Suppose that a college invests three-quarters of the required capital, a private investor provides the remainder, and a corporation is formed with a directorship consisting of persons who do not serve as members of the governing board of the college. The corporation establishes a video arcade in a shopping center, earns profits, and pays income tax on them. The after-tax profits are distributed to the owners (the college and the private investor) in the form of dividends. As long as the dividends do not exceed 35 percent of the total college revenues, its tax-exempt status is not threatened. Dividends are not subject to further tax because of the college's tax-exempt status. The source of the funds for the college's 75 percent share in the corporation is another question. California law, as interpreted in the regulations of the various counties, for example, requires community colleges to spend their resources for the purposes that appear in their official budgets and, more generally, for educational and other nonprofit activities of the district. Budgeting funds for a profit-making venture unrelated to the college's educational program may not be contrary to either California statutes or county regulations, but may nevertheless raise legal questions that would take a long time to resolve. An alternative way to make the investment is through the college's foundation. It, too, is a tax-exempt entity, but it is not prevented from investing and managing its funds as it sees fit, at least in California.

The situation is much less complex when the for-profit venture is substantively related to the nonprofit purposes of the college. Assume that a college decides to start a banquet and catering service, providing food for receptions, weddings, community gatherings, and the like. The food is prepared in the college cafeteria when its valuable assets would otherwise stand idle. Most important, the food is prepared by students enrolled in the college's culinary arts program. In this situation, participation by students as a part of their educational program links this project to the nonprofit purposes of the college. Unlike the arcade venture, which paid corporate income tax, the banquet service would pay no taxes on its profits.

For-profit ventures, both related and unrelated to the nonprofit purposes of a community college, could be organized and operated under the auspices of an existing college foundation. This approach has the advantage of utilizing a financial organization already available to most community colleges. The foundation, however, is not without problems: it is also a nonprofit organization subject to IRS regulations concerning profit-making activities. These include, as discussed, the need for a separate organization for the profit-making operation, with no overlapping directorates, and the requirement that profits earned not exceed 35 percent of the foundation's total revenues. Most community college foundations are fairly small, with modest revenues. A successful venture might easily produce profits that exceed 35 percent of the foundation's total revenues.

In the beginning, however, there is little risk. The college will most likely initiate enterprises related to its regular nonprofit purposes by employing assets already available on campus. Most significant, it will adopt generally accepted accounting practices to calculate its costs. This is an important feature of the for-profit venture. As with other public agencies, public community colleges have no asset or overhead accounting systems. As a result, the costs of programs do not take into account the depreciation of buildings, equipment, and other fixed assets, nor do they allow for reasonable allocations of employee benefits, utility and insurance costs, custodial services, and general administrative overhead. In an operation such as a banquet service, those indirect costs, when added to such direct costs as supplies, labor, advertising, and delivery, reduce paper profits substantially. They do not, however, reduce cash revenues attributable to the operation. Such revenues are thus considered a direct contribution to the institution.

Structural Organization of the Venture

Sooner or later, however, if the venture is successful, the issue of organization will become preeminent. At that point, the college will be well advised to organize its profit-making venture separately.

In summary, there are three primary alternatives:

1. Organize for-profit ventures unrelated to the college's nonprofit purpose. Establish a separate corporate organization for the ventures. Capitalize the corporation with funds from the college's foundation, with at least 20 percent of the capitalization from private investors.

2. Organize for-profit ventures related to the college's nonprofit purposes. Establish a separate corporate organization with financing from the college foundation and private investors, as in 1 above.

3. Organize for-profit ventures related to the college's nonprofit purposes. Because revenues from these ventures are nontaxable, the ventures may be operated directly by the college foundation. Limits on profits the IRS places on tax-exempt institutions and the constraint against overlapping directorates should be carefully observed.

Of these alternatives, 1 and 2 hold the most promise for the long run. Alternative 3 works fine as long as the enterprise does little more than break even. In that situation, the foundation serves as no more than a receiving agent for fees paid to the college for goods and services provided.

What Is Currently Happening

In an effort to ascertain the degree to which California community colleges were engaged in for-profit ventures as early as 1982, each district was sent a brief questionnaire. Of the seventy districts, thirty-six responded. Thirteen described activities they were either operating or planning to operate for a profit. It is safe to assume that the districts that did not respond are not engaged in revenue diversification ventures, even though they may be engaged in operations similar to those reported by the responding institutions. The following paragraphs summarize the types of positive responses.

Catering Food Service to the Community. Most community colleges have an elaborate food-preparation facility. Adding some equipment, perhaps, and scheduling operations at times when the facility is not preparing food for on-campus consumption makes it possible to take full advantage of valuable food-preparation assets. Santa Barbara Community College, for example, caters food to airlines at the Santa Barbara airport.

Retail Sales. In view of the heavy traffic on community college campuses, retail merchandising offers an exciting opportunity to generate revenue. College bookstores typically sell more than just books and school supplies, and there is no reason why the idea cannot be expanded. The Associated Students of Orange Coast College, for example, have operated a fashion store on campus for more than twenty-five years. For some time, Compton College has been operating a hospital gift shop.

Leasing Facilities and Granting Concessions. One would suspect that community colleges lease facilities and grant concessions to a great extent, although the responses to the questionnaire did not bear out that idea. Possibly these practices were not seen in the 1980s as profit-making in the same sense as contract instruction or retail sales. Nevertheless, the practice is probably widespread.

Conclusions

Successful revenue diversification for community colleges will take advantage of available physical assets that can be pressed into profit-making service. Kitchen equipment for a catering operation and a library for a computerized information-gathering service are ready examples. Successful ventures will also take advantage of opportunities and features peculiar to the institution. The College of the Siskiyous, for instance, is uniquely situated to sell log-wood homes and furniture and has a related instructional program.

Organizing and implementing for-profit activities will require considerable discussion, legal advice, and consultation with experts in business organization, taxation, accounting, and market research. It will also take managerial and business talent, particularly in the field of marketing. The appointment of a full-time business manager for revenue diversification activities is recommended. The college might have someone on staff who could undertake that responsibility—a person who knows what to do and how to do it.

Help is available. The Small Business Administration (SBA) and its Service Corps of Retired Executives (SCORE) in the SBA's Los Angeles office can provide a wealth of knowledge. Other sources of help and information include the American Federation of Small Business, Chicago; the Institute for New Enterprise Development, Belmont, Maine; the National Business League, Washington, D.C.; and the National Council for Small Business Development, Milwaukee.

The college board of trustees should review information about revenue diversification and, if so disposed, should make a commitment for a full-scale investigation of the opportunities within the district's resources. The following steps could then be taken:
1. Review by the college's top administrative staff
2. Establishment of a collegewide (or districtwide) steering committee consisting of both administrators and faculty
3. Identification of possible revenue diversification projects for further investigation by the steering committee
4. Establishment of consulting teams for each activity; the teams should include administrators, faculty, and advisers from the business community and should have expertise in the activity being investigated

5. Selection of two or three for-profit ventures to implement as pilot programs
6. Consultation with legal and tax experts for the purpose of establishing the best organizational and operational plan for the ventures
7. Start-up of the ventures
8. Evaluation of the ventures after one year of operation, to discover not so much how profitable they are as how well the diversification procedures work
9. Modification of procedures as needed. Continue by adding more for-profit ventures as the opportunities arise.

Revenue diversification will not solve college financial problems. Initial ventures are more likely to cover just costs and contribute a little to overhead than to earn significant profits. But even that contribution may make them worthwhile. Unlike the private business concern, which must risk considerable capital to go into business, community colleges can utilize existing assets in the form of both physical facilities and personnel, so that the risk can be minimized.

References

Barton, Stevens, and Masarsky, Ltd. "Higher Education Diversification Study." Unpublished manuscript, Barton, Stevens, and Massarsky, Ltd., Palo Alto, Calif., 1982.
Breneman, D. W., and Nelson, S. C. *Financing Community Colleges, an Economic Perspective.* Washington, D.C.: Brookings Institution, 1981.
Carnegie Council on Policy Issues in Higher Education. *Three Thousand Futures: The Next Twenty Years for Higher Education.* San Francisco: Jossey-Bass, 1980.
Friedrich, O. "Five Ways to Wisdom." *Time,* September 27, 1982, pp. 66-72.
Hopkins, B. "The Tax Implications of Profit-Making Ventures." *Grantsmanship Center News,* 1982, *10* (46), 38-41.
Mingle, J. R., and Associates. *Challenges of Retrenchment: Strategies for Consolidating Programs, Cutting Costs, and Reallocating Resources.* San Francisco: Jossey-Bass, 1981.
Williams, R. M. "Two That Made It and One That Didn't." *Grantsmanship Center News,* 1982a, *10* (46), 26-31.
Williams, R. M. "Why Don't We Set Up a Profit-Making Subsidiary?" *Grantsmanship Center News,* 1982b, *10* (45), 14-23.

Richard W. Brightman is director of educational services at Coast Community College District, Costa Mesa, California.

Commercial development of college land requires the deft hand of the college's board of trustees. Schoolcraft College has integrated the public and private sectors compatibly.

A Case for Commercial Development of College Property

Richard W. McDowell, W. Kenneth Lindner

Community college revenue has traditionally been limited to such sources as local property taxes, appropriations from state legislatures, tuition, and grants. Many colleges have also formed foundations to attract private-sector support in various forms, including gifts. Occasionally, colleges have tried other, somewhat less traditional means of generating revenues. One of these, the sale or leasing of college land, was attempted with significant success by Schoolcraft College in Livonia, Michigan.

Schoolcraft's twenty-five-year history, like that of many other community colleges in the country, is one of revenues that have not kept pace with institutional financial needs. Faced with the cost of modernizing instructional equipment and maintaining aging buildings, Schoolcraft also needed additional facilities to consolidate its student services areas and to move business services from temporary quarters. In light of these needs, Schoolcraft chose to allocate a portion of the college's land for commercial enterprise. This plan provided revenues sufficient to provide the college with a multimillion dollar endowment.

The plan was accomplished with minimal risk to the institution and represents yet another option for revenue generation available to community colleges.

Consideration of a New Concept

The commercial development of Schoolcraft College property was first proposed by a major airline that expressed interest in purchasing a portion of college land for a regional reservations center. Faced with this proposal, trustees conducted an intensive review of the implications of the idea of land development. They worked through each of these questions to determine whether or not to proceed:

1. Does the college own land that will not be needed in the future to accommodate enrollment growth, evolution of programs, or expanded college facilities?
2. Can the college legally use public land for private commercial enterprise?
3. To what degree do trustees see their role as holders of land as a public trust?
4. What will commercial development do to the campus environment?
5. Will the development project be successful?
6. What advantages will the development project offer the college?
7. How will anticipated revenues be utilized?

Updating the campus master plan was the first order of business, to determine whether any surplus land existed as well as the degree to which it could be turned over for noncollege use. Over several months, information was gathered about area demographics, projected student enrollment, anticipated additions and deletions to the curriculum, and the need for additional on- and off-campus facilities to accommodate these changes. When the trustees sat down to make their decision, they had a solid basis from which to project future needs.

The college then asked its legal counsel for an opinion about whether designated college land could be sold or leased and if so under what conditions. The attorney believed that if the college determined it had excess land, the land could be sold. If the land might be needed at some future time, however, then it would be better to develop it under a lease agreement.

When the first two concerns had been resolved, the issue turned to the effect sharing of land with a commercial enterprise would have on the college environment. After hearing presentations from developers on proposed uses for the property, the trustees came to some decisions: whatever the plan, the developer would have to assure the college of the development's potential success, enter into a contract that would guarantee revenues to the college, and stipulate that if at any point the project were to be abandoned, the land and all improvements would be returned to the college.

Ultimately, Schoolcraft trustees adopted the philosophy that college land is a capital asset, which, if it is to be utilized in an unconventional way, must generate significant revenue for site improvement or building expansion. The income from the development would be endowed and the interest earnings would be available to promote endeavors consistent with the college mission.

Formulation of the Plan

It was determined through the planning process that the college had seventeen acres of land located at the edge of the campus, adjacent to an interstate highway exit. That land was not immediately needed to fulfill the college's master plan, so trustees decided to make it available for development. The board began the public process by conducting a hearing to give citizens the opportunity to express concerns, if any, about proposed commercial development. The sparse attendance and lack of any real issues assured trustees that there were no major objections from the community.

Nevertheless, as elected representatives of the college district, Schoolcraft trustees saw the need to ensure the long-term interests of the institution and decided not to sell college property. After considerable discussion, it was agreed that the development project, if undertaken, should stipulate that the land would be leased rather than sold. That arrangement would allow for the option of returning the land and all its improvements to the college after a specified period of time.

To determine the relative benefits to the college of the lease arrangement, an income schedule was developed to indicate the annual and cumulative payments to the college, the interest income this money would earn if endowed, and the total balance in the endowment fund if no appropriations were made. This information was important in deciding how large the fund should be and in developing a plan for expenditures.

Formation of a Development Authority

The final order of business was the establishment of a development authority to shield the college from liability arising from the development and to permit income to be passed on to the college without tax consequences. Created on the advice of the college's legal counsel, this nonprofit, tax-exempt, private corporation, called the Schoolcraft Development Authority, was authorized under Michigan law. The college could be assured that long-term control would be maintained in the authority, because of the nine directors two were college trustees and three were college administrators. The authority's initial responsibility included selection of a developer, negotiating an option/development agreement, providing a survey of the property and a clear land title, approving plans for land use, providing for reciprocal easement agreements, and drawing up land leases for each phase of development.

Selection of a Developer

The trustees prepared a list of criteria that would minimize risk to the college in the selection of a developer:
- Unqualified recommendation from a major regional bank, the college attorney, and auditor
- Long-standing relationships with major financial institutions and the capacity to perform the obligation of a general partnership
- Demonstrated financial strength and the ability and willingness to commit its own resources to carry the project through to actuality
- Capacity to finance, supervise, design, construct, and manage the property
- Established fiduciary responsibility that can withstand the legal and ethical tests and act on behalf of the client
- Ability to perform, get results, and experience with joint ventures and projects over $30 million
- Demonstrated established management reputation, experience, and capability of controlling and managing a long-term project. Also, willingness to permit the college to review the resumé of the manager who would be assigned to the project
- Willingness to provide preliminary concepts for a land-utilization plan before a formal development relationship is established and, if selected, to present building renderings to the trustees for review before initiating any construction
- No competitive projects by the developer in the immediate geographic area.

The guidelines having been established, proposals from prospective developers were reviewed. Because of the publicity the college had received in the news media, twenty-nine companies requested additional information from the college about the intended use for the property. Each company was sent a request for proposals. Of the original twenty-nine, seven companies submitted proposals that were reviewed by staff. Four of these proposals were recommended for review by the board of trustees. The presentations were made, and the developers' concepts were discussed. The developer who was selected won support for his proposed use of land, the esthetics of the project, and the financial return to the college. This plan called for the construction of two office buildings, a hotel, and a restaurant and promised a greenbelt area to buffer the college from the project and provide proper esthetics.

Under the agreement, the developer accepted the obligation to plan, design, finance, construct, and manage the project. A $10 million letter of credit from a major lender was provided, and a timetable for starting and completing the project was guaranteed. In the agreement, four project development phases were identified, and options were established for each phase. The agreement further specified that the developer was to pay all real estate taxes and revenues to the college at the times and in the amounts specified. The development of each parcel would be controlled by a land sublease. Furthermore, the project would conform to all state and local codes and the lender would assume all obligations in case of abandonment by the developer. The agreement also stipulated that building systems must be upgraded periodically to prevent functional obsolescence and that the project could be sold or refinanced only with the approval of the authority.

Financial Considerations

The following specific financial considerations were established: (1) the college leases seventeen acres of land to the Schoolcraft Development Authority for a period of seventy-four years at a rate of $1 per year; (2) the authority, under the terms of the option/development agreement, subleases each parcel to the developer as scheduled; and (3) the financial terms provide for annual payments from the developer to the development authority on a quarterly basis and include the following.

- 2 percent of the land value of all undeveloped land (the land value is determined to be $150,000 per acre or $2.55 million for the total site)
- 10 percent of the land value as each option is exercised
- 0.75 percent of the adjusted gross income from the building leases (adjusted gross income allows for deduction of debt service only; the office leases are priced at a fixed value per square foot with economic adjustments every five years).

Benefits to College

Earnings from the project (shown in Table 1) are of obvious benefit to the college. Schoolcraft College will have many opportunities for improvement from the assurance of a major new income source over an extended period. As a result of this project, the college is contemplating the construction of a new building, to be accomplished without seeking additional millage or becoming dependent on the economic and political considerations usually associated with state funding. The financial self-

Table 1. Revenues from Land Development Project

Year	Annual Payments to College	Cumulative Payments to College	Interest Income from Endowment (8%)	Balance in Endowment Fund
5	$380,025	$ 1,003,450	$ 53,353	$ 1,100,290
10	333,148	2,709,482	244,424	3,632,861
15	425,191	4,642,377	530,640	7,588,831
20	542,663	7,109,296	998,568	14,023,338
25	692,590	10,257,778	1,746,582	24,271,454

sufficiency of the project creates pride and motivates the campus community to find other equally nontraditional approaches to generating income.

In this project diverse elements came together at the right time. The college is located in an area experiencing considerable commercial development; the project therefore enhances the value of the college's property. The college was able to identify prime land that was not needed immediately for college use. As a result, the college will experience a steady stream of income for many years. There may also be some synergistic relationships with the companies that move into the office buildings and with the hotel. The college may be able to find cooperative educational experiences and jobs for students with these companies. Such relationships are beneficial to the companies and help to promote the economic development of the area, to create new job opportunities, and to bring new tax revenues.

Words of Caution

Experience is a wonderful teacher, and there are some lessons that need to be considered before a college decides to initiate land development projects.

1. The institution should obtain professional legal and economic development advice if the resources are unavailable on campus.

2. There should be a review of state statutes to indicate if there are restrictions on the use of land holdings dedicated to higher education.

3. The college should be prepared to respond to the allegation that the developer, who is a partner with the college, has an unfair advantage in the competitive market because of the tax-exempt status of the college. This assumption is not true, because the developed property is added to the tax rolls and subject to real estate taxes, which are the developer's responsibility. The construction costs, the maintenance, and operation costs are fully charged to the developer and are similar to any private

development project. The initial advantage to the developer is in not having to buy the land, but that amount gets paid manyfold over the life of the contract.

4. The college may have to respond to complaints about the increased traffic and congestion from commercial development in the area. An appropriate response is to describe the economic impact of the project, including the generation of new jobs, as well as tax dollars to support local government and education.

5. The selection of the developer as a partner is very important. The long-term commitment between the college and the developer is analogous to marriage—both partners need to be satisfied with the arrangements.

6. The timing of a development is important with respect to the economic climate in the area. Marketing studies are helpful in predicting the need for commercial space. The developer will conduct the marketing research, since it is the developer's money and that of its investors that is at risk.

Community colleges frequently have limited revenue sources and certainly lack the research facilities and related resources of large universities. One asset, rarely developed, is land. Commercial development of that land can prove an important new revenue source.

Richard W. McDowell is president of Schoolcraft College, Livonia, Michigan.

W. Kenneth Lindner is former vice-president for business services at Schoolcraft College and president of the Schoolcraft Development Authority.

Higher education, especially at research universities, has long felt the economic impact of grant funds. For the community college, the performance contract may provide an equal opportunity for alternate funding.

Performance Contracting: Profits and Perils

Charles C. Spence, Jeffrey G. Oliver

Many community, junior, and technical colleges throughout the country have for some time been experiencing static or declining enrollments. The reasons include lower birthrates, increased competition from private trade schools, low unemployment rates, and changing district demographics. The net effect is reduced revenue in the face of escalating operating costs. Many institutions have reacted with layoffs, reduction of programs and services, and general retrenchment to traditional "bread and butter" courses and programs.

Faced with a similar problem, Florida Community College at Jacksonville (FCCJ) was able to reverse declining enrollments and turn a liability into an opportunity. That opportunity is performance contracting, which has allowed FCCJ to prosper both financially and programmatically, even to expand curriculum offerings and services. As the title of this chapter implies, performance contracting involves risk-taking. In fact, a review of performance contracts in California in 1986 revealed that one in five lost money for the contractor (Thor, 1987).

The purpose here is to share insights FCCJ has gained over several years by operating performance contracts effectively. Those insights are offered in hopes of reducing the risks to other community colleges.

Performance Contracts Versus Grants

Virtually all college administrators understand what a grant is. Unfortunately, that knowledge can work against them if they attempt to operate performance contracts as if they were grants. In fact, this misunderstanding can have, and has had, severe fiscal effects on colleges and even on administrators' careers.

Grants do have one advantage over performance contracts, inasmuch as they cover a much wider range of interests (see Table 1). For example, performance contracts are not generally available for transfer education or programs in the fine or performing arts. They are offered primarily for job training and employment, largely because of the influence of the Job Training Partnership Act (JTPA).

Availability

One aspect of performance contracting that makes it more attractive than grants is the availability of funding. The JTPA is a primary source

Table 1. Differences Between Grants and Performance Contracts

	Grants	*Performance Contracts*
Budget	Detailed line item budget required by funding agency.	Line item budget, if required by the funding agency, does not become part of the contract.
Objectives or goals	Frequently focus on process as well as product. Example: "Three faculty members will be updated in high technology areas CIM, CAM, CAD" (but "updated" is not defined in terms of outcomes.	Specific, quantifiable objectives with evidence of completion and time frames identified. Example: A student who completes thirty-two hours in the CAD program must be placed in a CAD-related job at $5.25/hour within sixty days of completion of course work.
Payment	Payment generally provided at regular intervals.	Usually no advance payment; payment only after objective is completed and delivered.
Excess funds	Returned to the funding agency.	Retained by the institution for reinvestment in the program.

of performance contracts, and nationally over twice as much funding is appropriated for the JTPA than for all of vocational education. In Florida, for example, the JTPA spent over $60 million during fiscal year 1987-88. At least $48 million of this funding was distributed directly to the twenty-four local service delivery areas (SDAs), many of which are Private Industry Councils. The vast majority of JTPA funding for Florida is on a local performance contracting basis. In 1987-88, FCCJ's success rate for securing JTPA funding via performance contracts from the local SDA was 100 percent. The college succeeded because it recognized these facts operationally: (1) it is much easier to pursue a contract from a local agency that controls several million dollars than it is to compete nationally for the same amount of money, and (2) performance contracting must be a high administrative priority to be successful.

Local performance contracting has become important to FCCJ's future, and it has also pursued state and federal performance contracts and grants. In fact, in 1988 FCCJ operated over a hundred performance contracts and grants, most of which were from state or federal agencies. The bottom line is this: time and resources allocated for additional funding are limited. These resources are most effective when spent in response to a request for proposal (RPF) from the local Private Industry Council than from the much more uncertain federal source. If local RFPs do not offer the opportunity needed to help the institution meet its goals, a state or federal performance contract or grant can be sought.

Flexibility and Accountability

Within the parameters of a request for proposal, performance contracts are usually flexible, especially about details of services to be provided. This flexibility is particularly apparent in budgeting. If the cost of the product (training) is acceptable to the funding agency, there are no conditions or stipulations on how the money may be spent. Once the contract is signed, however, the product must be produced exactly as written and within the specified time frames. This is the accountability side. In reality, the contract amount in a performance contract is a funding cap, rather than an award as in the case of a grant. If the institution does not produce the product agreed on, all costs incurred in the project become a liability for the institution.

In performance contracts, accountability is extremely high because payment is not made until the product is actually delivered. In a community college, the product often consists of a student placed in full-time employment for a minimum of thirty days on completion of a training program. Even if the institution recruits the student, determines eligibility, trains and counsels the student, pays the student's tuition, and provides him or her with child-care services, the institution is paid only for placement. If the student suddenly terminates employment after twenty-nine days to go to live with an aunt in Texas, the college receives no funding and may in fact be penalized in other ways. For example, if the training-related placement rate drops below 75 percent, the college may not be eligible for another contract the following year. In most states, including Florida, there is a 100 percent verification follow-up carried out directly with the employer on all placements by the state employment agency. This procedure is a double check on the placement documentation already submitted by the college, which contains the signatures of the student, a college representative, and the employer. Some employers object to the red tape and duplication of effort, but most accept the documentation requirement as something they have to put up with when working with the government.

To be truly accountable, one factor is needed: a clear line of authority. One person should be responsible for all performance contracts. That person must thoroughly understand the principles of performance contracting and the funding agencies' policies, procedures, and priorities.

The president of the college must understand that the dollars advanced by the institution to operate performance contracts are placed at risk. Unless the programs (contracts) are operated effectively and in a timely manner, the institution will lose money. Institutions are often advised to operate a program as a separate business instead of a college department or unit. The freestanding business of performance contracting can yield creative programs and services and excess income for reinvestment.

Neither the title of the person administering the performance contracting department nor its location within the institution is as important as central control and top administrative support. At FCCJ, the director of development and operations for performance contracting reports to the vice-president/provost of the downtown campus, who answers directly to the president.

Contract Operation

Performance contracts and grant programs are often written by, but rarely staffed by, the most creative employees in the college. Because the funding commitment is short term, established faculty and professionals avoid "soft money" positions. This attitude is certainly understandable, but it presents a real barrier to the successful operation of performance contracts. By their very nature, performance contracts are demanding, and they have strict time frames. No slack is allowed for time lost because of slow processing of personnel applications, requisitions, bids, or contracts. There is no substitute for the experienced manager who knows which buttons to push to expedite these processes. To alleviate the problem, FCCJ has created the position of contracts operations officer and filled it with one of the most successful program managers of the college. When a new performance contract begins at FCCJ, that person automatically becomes the manager of the new project until the contract is signed, staff is hired and trained, facilities and offices are established, equipment has been purchased, and the program is operating smoothly. The contracts operations officer is also involved with the planning and submission of new performance contracts, and therefore ensures that objectives are realistic. The position is funded out of several performance contracts and is not dependent on any particular one, which ensures that the stability and level of funding necessary for such a position are maintained.

Some Whys and Wherefores

Like most community colleges in the nation, FCCJ lists promoting the success of students among its mission objectives. Performance contracting enhances the college's ability to meet that goal. It seems reasonable to assume that most colleges could use performance contracting to support their institutional objectives, because it allows the institution to provide high-quality, high-cost services to the poorest and least employable members of the community. Over the last several years, FCCJ has attracted $2.5 million to support special programs for persons with disabilities, the elderly, displaced homemakers, high school dropouts, the long-term unemployed, and the economically disadvantaged.

These programs have had a dramatic impact on hundreds of lives. One example is Donny, who graduated from FCCJ's Computer Programmer Training for Disabled Students project. Donny is a bright man with severe cerebral palsy. He uses a wheelchair, and his speech is difficult to understand. After fifteen years of services from various state agencies, Donny had acquired two bachelor of science degrees (at a cost of over $20,000 in public monies) and still had not been on a job interview. FCCJ and its business advisory committee changed that. Not only did Donny get a job interview, he was hired by Prudential Insurance Company at a starting salary of over $20,000 a year. After nearly two years, Donny had been promoted and was well on his way to earning $30,000 a year. Funding, partially provided by a JTPA Title III performance contract, enabled Donny to go to work and live independently.

Although much attention has been paid to performance contracts acquired from JTPA and the Private Industry Council, it also should be noted that FCCJ has provided services to the Department of Defense (Navy), Department of Corrections, Florida Department of Health and Rehabilitative Services, and Florida Department of Education through various performance contracts. In some cases, the college has provided services to agencies with special needs rather than to special needs populations. For example, FCCJ was awarded a Department of Defense (DOD) contract to produce the DANTES (Defense Activity for NonTraditional Education Support) catalogue for Education and Resource Centers. This publication is an exhaustive catalogue of educational materials, supplies, and equipment that would help military personnel set up learning centers on any U.S. military installation in the world, including ships at sea. Lessons learned in producing two successful DANTES catalogues led to FCCJ's being awarded the National Home Study Council Guide contract. This guide enabled Navy personnel to obtain credit for courses through extensive examination and independent study programs offered worldwide. Navy personnel have earned credentials ranging from high school diplomas to graduate degrees. As well as generating nearly $2 million in additional enrollments, these contracts have directly paid $267,000 in tuition and $140,000 in books and equipment and netted the college a surplus of $163,000 after all direct expenses.

Keys to Developing Proposals

The request for proposal usually spells out the eligibility criteria and outcomes required by the funding agency. This leaves the school that is awarded the contract a wide latitude to develop service delivery techniques and program configurations. Generally RFPs will request documentation of community need of the programs and services to be offered. It is essential for the performance contracting department to have direct access to the college's institutional research staff and related outside agencies, such as the state job service, so these needs can be properly documented.

Proposals developed for performance contracts should not be embellished (as in grant applications), because the proposal may become part of the contract. "Wiggle room" should be in the proposal wherever possible, however. For example, if the proposal is to train word processors and the training takes a maximum of 300 hours, the college should not state that the students will receive 300 hours of training. If that statement becomes part of the contract, any student not receiving 300 documented hours of training will be disallowed for payment. Observe this rule of thumb: always be prepared to document everything you commit to in the proposal, because you will be audited and monitored for precise program compliance.

Contractors should be particularly cautious about optimistic time frames. Adequate time to start up programs should be provided. Advertising for and hiring staff, ordering equipment, establishing offices, and recruiting students often take more time than the inexperienced contractor projects.

Contract Monitoring

The process described above produces the need for a contract compliance officer who will be responsible for collecting data, monitoring, reporting, and overall contract compliance.

Monitoring and follow-up are especially critical in performance contracting, because without proper reporting the contractor will not be paid. The contract compliance officer or contract manager must develop procedures with the business department to ensure that performance is reported to the funding agency, on the proper forms, and within the designated time frames. Feedback from the finance department must be reviewed regularly to make sure proper payment has been made for the activities reported. The finance department may receive a check from the funding agency with no explanation of its purpose. Coordination between the contract manager and finance department is essential to establish a clear audit trail and to interpret transactions.

The contract compliance officer or program manager must also review the financial status of the program regularly to make timely decisions about staffing. With contracts, unlike grants, the only way to cut losses if proposed standards of performance are not being achieved is to cut expenses, usually staff. There can be no tenure obligation with performance contracts.

Caveats: Anatomy of a Loser

Careful analysis of the performance contracts operated by FCCJ that have lost money indicates several points that deserve further elaboration. If the reader follows the suggestions made earlier in this chapter, most of these problems will never arise; but the importance of clarity at this point outweighs the danger of repetition.

The four major problems FCCJ has experienced in performance contracting are (1) failing to understand student motivation, (2) insufficient planning, (3) fragmented administrative responsibility, and (4) lack of operational experience with performance contracting.

Student motivation sounds like a simple thing to deal with until one considers all the issues, such as disincentives to work. Members of the special needs populations that training and employment programs are designed to serve are often difficult to motivate to persist in working. Unemployment or veteran's benefits, workers' compensation, social security, Medicare, Medicaid, food stamps, welfare, subsidized housing, and a myriad of other agency benefits may be difficult, even for a motivated person, to give up in order to go to work. Project planning must include not only the best interests and priorities of the college, the funding agency, and potential employers, but also the specific characteristics and conditions of the target population. The long-term unemployed, dropouts, displaced homemakers, economically disadvantaged persons and those with disabilities all have unique problems that can be disincentives to employment and must be addressed.

In Florida, for example, research indicates that the average recipient of Aid to Families with Dependent Children (AFDC) in 1987 had to make $6.05 an hour working to equal the welfare benefits. Working for fast-food chains at well below that rate will not attract AFDC recipients. More to the point, a training program for word processing operators starting at $5.00 an hour in 1987 would probably not succeed if it had aimed at AFDC recipients.

Insufficient planning may occur in many cases because reliable data do not exist. Recognizing this common problem, the performance contracting department, as a part of the strategic planning process at FCCJ in 1987, requested funding to collect relevant data. Unless special attention is given to research, performance contracts will be lost.

Fragmented responsibility, as described earlier, can also lead to the downfall of a project. At FCCJ, the director of development and operations for performance contracting is responsible, as the title implies, for the development, implementation, operation, and follow-up of all performance contracts regardless of the type of training or the target population. Centralizing authority eliminates ambiguity of control and evaluation. At FCCJ, performance contracts, like all grants, used to be managed by the most closely affiliated administrator. Theoretically, it makes sense for a performance contract to train displaced homemakers in word processing to be supervised by the dean of business programs. The dean of business, however, without many hours of training and constant refreshers, will be unlikely to manage a performance contract effectively. The performance contract will become a large and time-consuming problem, one quite foreign to that person's responsibility.

A classic example of responsibility's falling through the cracks is a performance contract that trained students for a year and placed them in high-paying computer programmer jobs averaging around $20,000 a year. The contract was properly performed; the placements, however, were made two days after the contract expired, resulting in a loss to FCCJ of more than $10,000.

The last major pitfall is the lack of understanding of how performance contracts operate. As discussed throughout this chapter, performance contracts do not allow time for the normal learning curve most of us need. Funding agencies are not forgiving. The contract is usually specific. Either you perform or you do not. The JTPA is built on the business model. At least 51 percent of the policymakers must by law come from the private sector. It is therefore unrealistic for educators to expect anything but a straightforward business approach to the management of these contracts.

In March 1989, the final regulations were published in the Federal Register, which changed the process for negotiating contracts and the way profits from program income can be utilized.

Reference

Thor, L. M. "Performance Contracting: Successfully Managing Risk." In W. W. Wilms and R. W. Moore (eds.), *Marketing Strategies for Changing Times.* New Directions for Community Colleges, no. 60. San Francisco: Jossey-Bass, 1987.

Charles C. Spence is president of Florida Junior College, Jacksonville.

Jeffrey G. Oliver is assistant dean for employment and training programs at Florida Junior College, Jacksonville.

APPENDIX 1
A Guide to Key Resources

Alumni Giving

Jennifer Kerns (1986) and her organization, the Junior and Community College Institute (1986), have produced two excellent articles on alumni fund raising. The institute's paper deals with the potential for alumni giving and systematically with the "it won't work" myths that are prevalent today. Kerns covers a wide range of programmatic options available for institutions that choose to develop alumni as a resource. Rock (1981) describes a case study of an alumni program that was widely regarded as a model in the early 1980s.

Junior and Community College Institute. *Two-Year College Alumni: An Untapped Resource.* Washington, D.C.: Junior and Community College Institute, 1986. 162 pp. (ED 278 457)

Kerns, J. R. *Two-Year College Alumni Programs into the 1990s.* Washington, D.C.: Junior and Community College Institute, 1986. (ED 277 435)

Kopecek, R. J. *The Alumni—An Untapped Reservoir of Support.* Danvers, Mass.: National Council on Community Services and Continuing Education, 1980. 17 pp. (ED 195 317)

Kopecek, R. J., and Kubik, S. M. "Opportunities for Alumni Relations." In P. S. Bryant and J. A. Johnson (eds.), *Advancing the Two-Year College.* New Directions for Institutional Advancement, no. 15. San Francisco: Jossey-Bass, 1982.

McCracken, J. E., and others. *Community/Junior College Alumni: Initiative, Influence, and Impact.* San Francisco: American Association of Community and Junior Colleges, 1980. 11 pp. (ED 190 171)

Rock, T. L. "An Alumni Program That Brings Results." In J. E. Bennett (ed.), *Building Voluntary Support for Two-Year Colleges.* Washington, D.C.: Council for the Advancement and Support of Education, 1979.

Slabaugh, D. E. "Serving Diverse Alumni." In J. E. Bennett (ed.), *Building Voluntary Support for the Two-Year College.* Washington, D.C.: Council for the Advancement and Support of Education, 1979.

Stoddard, R. L. "Alumni and Fund Raising in the Rural Community College." In W. H. Sharron, Jr. (ed.), *The Community College Foundation.* Washington, D.C.: National Council for Resource Development, 1982.

Case Studies of Success

Angel and Gares (1981) present data accumulated in a nationwide survey that detail the characteristics of successful fund-raising programs at nine community colleges. Graham (1983) and Weidenthal (1982) offer institutional case studies that explain specific programs and levels of resource commitment.

Angel, D., and Gares, D. "Profile of Nine Community Colleges with Successful Foundations." *Community and Junior College Journal,* 1981, *52,* 7-8.

Bock, D. E., and Sullins, R. W. "The Search for Alternative Funding: Community Colleges and Private Fund Raising." *Community College Review,* 1987, *15,* 13-20.

Graham, F. R., *Making Foundations Work.* Richmond: Virginia State Board for Community Colleges, 1983. 9 pp. (ED 255 254)

Higbee, J. M., and Stoddard, R. L. "Paving the Way to Prosperity." *Community and Junior College Journal,* 1981, *52* (2), 21-23.

Lake, D. B. "Founding a Foundation: A Mini Case Study." *Community and Junior College Journal,* 1981, *52,* 21-23.

Olivanti, R. A. "Founding a College Foundation: A Mini Case Study." *Community Service Catalyst,* 1983, *13,* 14-16.

Tidewater Community College Educational Foundation. *Guidelines Manual for Fund Raising and Donations.* Portsmouth, Va.: Tidewater Community College Educational Foundation, 1983. 104 pp. (ED 243 551)

Webb, R. D., and Jackson, R. J. "Teaming Up for Resource Development." *Community and Junior College Journal,* 1979, *50,* 40-41.

Weidenthal, M. B. "Beating the Odds in Ohio." *Community and Junior College Journal,* 1982, *53,* 44-47.

Corporate Giving

Kendrick (1979) describes how a case for private giving can be made by demonstrating to corporations that community colleges save corporations time and money. Pokrass (1986, 1988) details specific ways in which community colleges can assess and cultivate corporate giving projects.

Ballard, W. J. "It's All in the Community: Community Colleges Can Win Corporate Support." *CASE Currents,* 1981, *10,* 42-43.

Green, J. "For Foothill College: Corporate Partnerships Are Win-Win Situations." *AGR Reports,* 1985, *17,* 30-32.

Kendrick, D. A. "Foundations and Corporations: National Resources for Your College." In J. E. Bennett (ed.), *Building Voluntary Support for the Two-Year College.* Washington, D.C.: Council for the Advancement and Support of Education, 1979.

Milligan, F. G. "Corporate Solicitation—SUNY Style: A Two-Year Urban Campus' Approach to Corporate Giving." Paper presented at the State University of New York's Conference "A Perspective on Corporate Giving," Corning, N.Y., Nov. 9, 1982. 13 pp. (ED 225 625)

Moore, G. E. "Corporate and Foundation Support for Public Institutions." In M. J. Worth (ed.), *Public College and University Development: Fund Raising at State Universities, State Colleges and Community Colleges.* Washington, D.C.: Council for the Advancement and Support of Education, 1985.

Pokrass, R. J. "A Study of Corporate Giving Behavior Toward Two-Year Colleges." Unpublished paper, Aug. 1986.

Pokrass, R. J. "Corporate Giving to Two-Year Colleges." *Currents,* Jan. 1988, pp. 38-40.

Establishing a Foundation

Sharron (1978, 1982a, 1982b) and Woodbury (1973, 1979, 1980) give the basics of building foundations at community colleges. Woodbury is excellent at presenting specific steps and the chronology of those actions. Sharron is best on building the board of directors, answering the problematic question why give to a public community college, and the identification of specific fund-raising program objectives.

Johnson, R. P. "The Community College Foundation and the Internal Revenue Service: Establishing and Maintaining Exempt Organization Status." In W. H.

Sharron, Jr. (ed.), *The Community College Foundation*. Washington, D.C.: National Council on Resource Development, 1982.

Nusz, P. J. *Development of Guidelines for Establishment and Operation of a California Community College Foundation.* Fort Lauderdale, Fla.: Nova University, 1986. 75 pp. (ED 273 315)

Robertson, A. J. "The Role of the Community College Foundation." In W. H. Sharron, Jr. (ed.), *The Community College Foundation*. Washington, D.C.: National Council for Resource Development, 1982.

Robison, S. "The Development of the Two-Year College Foundation and Techniques for Success." In W. H. Sharron, Jr. (ed.), *The Community College Foundation*. Washington, D.C.: National Council for Resource Development, 1982.

Sharron, W. H., Jr. *The Development and Organization of the Community College Foundation.* Resource Paper no. 18. Washington, D.C.: National Council for Resource Development, 1978.

Sharron, W. H., Jr. (ed.). *The Community College Foundation*. Washington, D.C.: National Council for Resource Development, 1982a.

Sharron, W. H., Jr. "Planning and Implementing the Foundation." In *The Community College Foundation*. Washington, D.C.: National Council for Resource Development, 1982b.

Silvera, A. L. "The Design and Utilization of Non-Profit Foundations Affiliated with California Community Colleges." Doctoral dissertation, University of Southern California, 1976.

Sims, L. M. "The College-Related Foundation as a Viable Concept for Resource Development in Alabama." Doctoral dissertation, University of Alabama, 1973.

Wattenbarger, J. L. "The Case for the Community College Foundation." In W. H. Sharron, Jr. (ed.), *The Community College Foundation*. Washington, D.C.: National Council for Resource Development, 1982.

Woodbury, K. B., Jr. "Community College Foundation." *Community and Junior College Journal*, 1973, *43*, 16-17, 48.

Woodbury, K. B., Jr. "How to Establish a College Foundation." In *Building Voluntary Support for the Two-Year College*. Washington, D.C.: Council for the Advancement and Support of Education, 1979.

Woodbury, K. B., Jr. "Establishing a Foundation." *CASE Currents*, 1980, *6*, 18-21.

Executive Director's Role

Gross (1982) outlines the technical, human, and conceptual skills necessary to an effective executive director. Garlock and McKee (1986) present an interesting test for determining where an executive places himself or herself on the continuum of needs. Mays's (1985) dissertation quantifies the most prevalent characteristics of development officers.

Garlock, J., and McKee, F. (1986). *Values and the Development Office*. Washington, D.C.: National Council for Resource Development, 1986.

Gross, E. K. "The Role of the Executive Director." In W. H. Sharron, Jr. (ed.), *The Community College Foundation*. Washington, D.C.: National Council on Resource Development, 1982.

Mays, S. B. "The Characteristics, Functions, Behaviors and Effectiveness of Development Officers in American Public Community Colleges." Unpublished doctoral dissertation, Virginia Polytechnic and State University, 1985.

Mays, S. A., and Vogler, D. E. "The Linkage Between Community Services and College Development." *Community Services Catalyst*, 1985, *15*, 10-13.

Rowh, M. *Leadership for the Development Function in the Two-Year College.* Greenville, S.C.: Greenville Technical College, 1987. (ED 278 459)

Webb, R. D., and Jackson, R. J. "Resource Development and Lake Land College." *Community College Review,* 1978, *6,* 34-36.

Nonfinancial Roles of the Foundation

Henry's (forthcoming) dissertation describes the importance of the various marketing roles of the foundation. Keener (1982) shows that the foundation's role in institutional planning, community improvement, and faculty enrichment goes beyond fund raising.

Blanshard, P., Jr. "Establishing Foundation Aids Community College's Service." *Fund Raising Management,* 1978, *7,* 40-43, 57.

Henry, E. "The Relative Value and Importance of Perceived Benefits of Active Foundations of Public Community Colleges in the United States." Unpublished doctoral dissertation, University of North Texas, forthcoming.

Keener, B. J. "The Foundation's Role in Resource Development." In W. H. Sharron, Jr. (ed.), *The Community College Foundation.* Washington, D.C.: National Council for Resource Development, 1982.

Mays, S. A., and Vogler, D. E. "The Linkage Between Community Services and College Development." *Community Services Catalyst,* 1985, *15,* 10-13.

Slabaugh, D. E. "How a College Foundation Can Boost Your Development Effort." In J. E. Bennett (ed.), *Building Voluntary Support for the Two-Year College.* Washington, D.C.: Council for the Advancement and Support of Education, 1979.

President's Role

Fisher's (1982) rules for presidential involvement guide the president who has not yet become immersed in fund raising. Robertson (1979) gives the perspective from the president's chair. Schulze's (forthcoming) dissertation proves that presidential involvement often translates into success in fund raising.

Fisher, J. L. "The Two-Year College President and Institutional Advancement." In P. S. Bryant and J. A. Johnson (eds.), *Advancing the Two-Year College.* New Directions for Institutional Advancement, no. 15. San Francisco: Jossey-Bass, 1982.

Robertson, A. J. "A Development Primer for Community Colleges." In J. E. Bennett (ed.), *Building Voluntary Support for the Two-Year College.* Washington, D.C.: Council for the Advancement and Support of Education, 1979.

Schulze, C. "The Role of the Community College President in Successful Fund Raising." Unpublished doctoral dissertation, Teachers College, Columbia University, forthcoming.

Sims, H. D. "The President as Money Manager." *Community and Junior College Journal,* 1978, *48,* 20-24.

Public Colleges and Private Giving

Stetson (1984) presents a valuable historical perspective on private giving to community colleges, complemented by Ryan (1987), who debunks the popular myths of the unacceptability of private fund raising at community colleges. Polk (1979) forthrightly presents the case for private giving to community colleges.

Bennett, J. E. (ed.). *Building Volunteer Support for the Two-Year College: How-to Information on Fund Raising, Community Relations, News/Information and Government Relations.* Washington, D.C.: Council for the Advancement and Support of Education, 1979.

Bremer, F. H., and Elkins, F. S. "Private Financial Support of Junior Colleges." *Junior College Journal,* 1965, *36,* 16-19.

Edison, R. "Community College Foundations: Advantages and Disadvantages." *Selected Papers for the Northern Illinois University Community College Conferences, 1967-68.* DeKalb, Ill.: DeKalb Community College Services, 1968.

Gragg, W. L., and Hessenflow, D. "Is There a Foundation in Your Future?" *Community College Frontiers,* 1979, *7,* 31-32.

Kopecek, R. J. "An Idea Whose Time Is Come: Not-for-Profit Foundations for Community Colleges." *Community College Review,* 1983, *10,* 12-17.

Kuhn, E. J. "Definition and Functions of the Community College Foundation." *Selected Papers from the Northern Illinois University Community College Conference, 1967-68.* DeKalb, Ill.: DeKalb Community College Services, 1968.

Polk, C. H. "Why Public Colleges Need Private Funds." In J. E. Bennett (ed.), *Building Voluntary Support for the Two-Year College.* Washington, D.C.: Council for the Advancement and Support of Education, 1979.

Ryan, G. J. "Guidelines for Effective Prospect Development." Paper presented at the 18th annual convention of the Association of Community College Trustees, Orlando, Fla., Oct. 1987.

Sims, H. D. "Private Funding Through Public Support." *Community College Journal,* 1976, *47,* 30-31.

Stetson, N. E. *The Development of a Historical Perspective on Private Financial Support for Public Two-Year Colleges.* Fort Lauderdale, Fla.: Nova University, 1984. 28 pp. (ED 253 287)

Wattenbarger, J. L. *The Role of the Professional Educator as the College Development Officer.* Washington, D.C.: National Council for Resource Development, 1975. 11 pp. (ED 203 919)

Wattenbarger, J. L. "Grantsmanship and the Community Junior College." *Peabody Journal of Education,* 1976, *53,* 166-170.

Worth, M. J. (ed.). *Public Colleges and University Development: Fund Raising at State Universities, State Colleges, and Community Colleges.* Washington, D.C.: Council for the Advancement and Support of Education, 1985.

Revenue Enhancement Role

Bailey (1986) reports on the significant increase in aggressive fund raising by community colleges. Palmer (1984) reviews the recent literature dealing with private financial development at community colleges.

Bailey, A. L. "Their Budgets Cut, Two-Year Colleges Turn to Aggressive Fund Raising." *Chronicle of Higher Education,* 1986, *33,* 57, 60.

Bock, D. E., and Sullins, W. R. "The Search for Alternative Funding: Community Colleges and Private Fund Raising." *Community College Review,* 1987, *15,* 13-20.

Brightman, R. W. "Revenue Diversification: A New Source of Funds for Community Colleges." Unpublished manuscript, 1982. 24 pp. (ED 221 251)

Degerstedt, L. M. "Non-Profit Foundations Formed by Public Community Colleges: Profile of Their Use for External Funding." Doctoral dissertation, Brigham Young University, 1979.

Graham, S., and Anderson, D. "Sources of Financing for Community Colleges." *Community College Review*, 1985, *13*, 50-56.

Hunt, S. *New Sources of Revenue: An Idea Book.* Washington, D.C.: Council for the Advancement and Support of Education, 1984.

Luck, M. F. "Educational Foundations—Alternative Development Strategies: Insurance for a Solvent Community College System." Paper presented at the annual convention of the American Association of Community and Junior Colleges, Denver, Colo., 1977.

Luck, M. F. "Foundations and Fund Raising in Public Community Colleges." *Fund Raising Management*, 1976, *7*, 12-17.

Luck, M. F., and Tolle, D. J. *Community College Development: Alternative Fund-Raising Strategies.* Indianapolis, Ind.: Rand R. Newkirk, 1978.

Luskin, B. J., and Warren, I. K. "Strategies for Generating New Financial Resources." In D. Campbell (ed.), *Strengthening Financial Management.* New Directions for Community Colleges, no. 50. San Francisco: Jossey-Bass, 1985.

Ottley, A. "Funding Strategies for Community Colleges." Paper presented at the Advanced Institutional Development Program Two-Year College Consortium, Central YMCA Community College, Chicago, 1978.

Palmer, J. "Alternative Funding for Community Colleges: An ERIC Review." *Community Services Catalyst*, 1984, *14*, 23-25.

Robison, S. "The Development of the Two-Year College Foundation and Techniques for Success." In W. H. Sharron, Jr. (ed.), *The Community College Foundation.* Washington, D.C.: National Council for Resource Development, 1982.

Stoudt, F. D. "The Untapped Source of Revenue." In J. Lombardi (ed.), *Meeting the Financial Crisis.* New Directions for Community Colleges, no. 2. San Francisco: Jossey-Bass, 1973.

Special Funding Programs

Behrendt (1984), Burke (1981), and Kiefler (1984) each discuss special programs that were funded through private giving at community colleges.

Behrendt, R. L. "Honors Programs and Private Funding: How One Community College Succeeded." Paper presented at the annual convention of the American Association of Community and Junior Colleges, Washington, D.C., April 1984. 15 pp. (ED 244 682)

Burke, T. "Using Innovative Fund Raising to Create a Campus." *Community and Junior College Journal*, 1981, *52*, 12-15.

Kiefler, J. "Foundation Faculty Fellowships Find Real World." *Community and Junior College Journal*, 1984, *54*, 33-34.

Criteria for Success

Duffy (1979, 1980, 1982) is the acknowledged expert in characteristics of successful foundations. That work has recently been complemented by Glandon (1987), Hollingsworth (1983a, 1983b), and Johnson (1986). Ryan and Smith (1987) researched characteristics of success present in the top ten fund-raising community colleges.

Duffy, E. F. "Evaluative Criteria for Community College Foundation." Doctoral dissertation, University of Florida, 1979.

Duffy, E. F. *Characteristics and Conditions of a Successful Community College Foun-*

dation. Washington, D.C.: National Council for Resource Development, 1980. 13 pp. (ED 203 918)

Duffy, E. F. "Characteristics and Conditions of a Successful Community College Foundation." In W. H. Sharron, Jr. (ed.), *The Community College Foundation.* Washington, D.C.: National Council on Resource Development, 1982.

Evans, N. D. "Diagnosing a Foundation: Ways to Put New Life into Your Foundation." *Community, Technical and Junior College Journal,* 1986, *52,* 27-30.

Glandon, B. L. "Critical Components of Successful Two Year College Foundations." Unpublished doctoral dissertation, Brigham Young University, 1987.

Hellweg, S. A. "Requisites for an Effective College Grants Development Operation." *Community College Review,* 1980, *8* (2), 5-12.

Hollingsworth, P. "An Investigation of Characteristics of Successful Community College Foundations." Unpublished doctoral dissertation, Pepperdine University, 1983a.

Hollingsworth, P. "An Investigation of Characteristics of Successful Community College Foundations." Graduate seminar paper, Pepperdine University, 1983b. 25 pp. (ED 233 756)

Johnson, J. J. "A Profile of Selected High- and Low- Performing Non-Profit Foundations in Public Community, Technical and Junior Colleges in the United States." Unpublished doctoral dissertation, Virginia Polytechnic Institute and State University, 1986.

Luck, M. F. "The Characteristics of Foundations and Fund Raising in Public Comprehensive Two-Year Colleges." Doctoral dissertation, University of Southern Illinois, 1974.

Luck, M. F. "Model Analyses of Community College Foundations: New Era." *Fund Raising Management,* 1977, *9,* 22-29.

McNamara, D. L. "The Roles of Institutional Personnel Connected with an Effective Two-Year College Private Fund Raising Program." Unpublished doctoral dissertation, Oklahoma State University, 1988.

Ryan, G. J., and Smith, N. J. "Characteristics of Success in Community College Fund Raising." Paper presented at the 67th annual convention of the American Association of Community and Junior Colleges, Dallas, Tex., Apr. 1987.

Smith, N. J. "Organizational Models of Successful Advancement Programs." Paper presented at the Annual Conference on Advancing Two-Year Institutions, Council for the Advancement and Support of Education, Alexandria, Va., December 9-11, 1986. 32 pp. (ED 278 435)

Strategies for Fund Raising

Walters (1987) describes all the forms of fund raising commonly used by community colleges. McNamara's (forthcoming) dissertation includes ratings of effectiveness of each fund-raising method by successful community colleges. Beckes (1982) and Bender and Edwards (1986) present the possibilities of sophisticated planned giving opportunities.

Beckes, I. K. "Gifts and Bequests for the Two-Year College Foundation." In W. H. Sharron, Jr. (ed.), *The Community College Foundation.* Washington, D.C.: National Council for Resource Development, 1982.

Bender, L., and Daniel, D. "Rethinking Funding Strategies." *Community Technical and Junior College Journal,* 1986, *57,* 22-25.

Conrad, L., Davis, B., Duffy, E., and Whitehead, J. "What Can Community Colleges Do to Increase Private Giving?" *Community, Technical and Junior College Journal,* 1986, *57* (2), 34-37.

Danbury, C. "Strategy for Fund Raising When You Are the New Kid on the Block." *Community and Junior College Journal*, 1981, *52*, 10-11.

Daniel, D. E. *Future Trends for Resource Development*. Research Report no. 35. Washington, D.C.: National Council for Resource Development, 1985.

Davidson, M. M., and Wise, S. R. "Fund Raising: The Public Two-Year College." In P. S. Bryant and J. A. Johnson (eds.), *Advancing the Two-Year College*. New Directions for Institutional Advancement, no. 15. San Francisco: Jossey-Bass, 1982.

Degerstedt, L. M. "The Strategies and Perceptions of Community Colleges and the Foundation: A National Perspective." In W. H. Sharron, Jr. (ed.), *The Community College Foundation*. Washington, D.C.: National Council on Resource Development, 1982.

Luck, M. F. "Foundations and Fund Raising in Public Community Colleges." *Fund Raising Management*, 1976, *7*, 12-17.

Luck, M. F. "Educational Foundations—Alternative Development Strategies: Insurance for a Solvent Community College System." Paper presented at the annual convention of the American Association of Community and Junior Colleges, Denver, Colo., April 1977.

Luck, M. F., and Tolle, D. J. *Community College Development: Alternative Fund-Raising Strategies*. Indianapolis, Ind.: Rand R. Newkirk, 1978.

McCain, J. C. *Resource Development Programs in Two-Year Colleges: A National Survey*. Washington, D.C.: National Council on Resource Development, 1975.

McNamara, D. L. "The Effective and/or Successful Characteristics of a Two-Year College Private Fund Raising Program." Unpublished doctoral dissertation, Oklahoma State University, forthcoming.

Nicksick, T., Jr. "The Special Purpose Foundation: Capital Fund." In W. H. Sharron, Jr. (ed.), *The Community College Foundation*. Washington, D.C.: National Council for Resource Development, 1982.

Ryan, G. J. "Guidelines for Effective Prospect Development." Paper presented at the 18th annual convention of the Association of Community College Trustees, Orlando, Fla., Oct. 1987.

Smith, N. J. "Gifts of Time, Talent . . . and Money." *Community and Junior College Journal*, 1981, *52*, 21-23.

Walters, L. *Dollars Equal the Margin of Excellence*. Decatur, Ga.: Southern Association of Community and Junior Colleges, 1987. 6 pp. (ED 281 600)

Trustees and Foundation Boards

Crowson's (1985) dissertation is the most recent study of the role of the volunteer board in fund raising. Sader (1986) amplifies Crowson's work through a study of the involvement of elected trustees in fund raising.

Bryant, D. W. "Organization of Community College Foundation Boards." *Community Junior College Quarterly of Research and Practice*, 1988, *12*, 65-71.

Crowson, J. "Boards of Directors of Community College Foundations: Characteristics, Roles, and Success." Unpublished doctoral dissertation, University of Mississippi, 1985.

Edwards, J. E., and Bender, L. W. *Women and Community College Foundations: Status, Myths and Insights*. Tallahassee: Tallahassee Institute for Studies in Higher Education, Florida State University, 1983. 50 pp. (ED 229 095)

Sader, C. H. *The Role of Elected Trustees of Public Institutions in Successful Development Programs*. Chicago: North Central Association of Colleges and Schools, 1986. 7 pp. (ED 266 841)

Policies of Major Philanthropies in the United States

The following is a list of 190 corporations and foundations, their key contact people, their addresses, and their policies regarding community college giving.

It is important to note that a "yes" does not mean the institution will accept proposals from all 1,200 community colleges. Most companies and foundations give grants within limited geographical areas. Many companies and foundations give only for specified purposes. Very careful research into the giving history and priorities of each institution should precede the submission of any proposal.

Equally important, a "no" does not mean that a community college should avoid an institution if the two appear to have interests in common.

Name/ Address	Contact/ Title/Phone	*Accepts Community College Proposals*
Aetna Life & Casualty Co. 151 Farmington Avenue Hartford, CT 06156	Sanford Cloud, Jr. Vice-President and Executive Director 203/273-3340	Yes
Ahmanson Foundation 9215 Wilshire Boulevard Beverly Hills, CA 90210	Lee Walcott Vice-President 213/278-0770	Yes
Allied Signal, Inc. Box 2245R Morristown, NJ 07960	Gail McKinney Manager 201/455-5876	Yes
Amerada Hess Corp. 1185 Avenue of the Americas New York, NY 10036	Christine Cangelosi Secretary, Contribution Committee 212/997-8500	No
American Express Co. American Express Foundation American Express Plaza World Financial Center New York, NY 10004	Mary Beth Salerno Vice-President and Director 212/640-5660	Yes
American Information Technology Corp. Ameritech Foundation 30 S. Wacker Drive Chicago, IL 60606	Michael Kuhlin Executive Director 312/750-5000	No
American Stores Co. Acme Markets, Inc. 124 N. 15th Street Philadelphia, PA 19101	Bob Neslund President 215/568-3000	No

American Telephone and Telegraph Co. AT&T Foundation 550 Madison Avenue, Room 2717 New York, NY 10022	Anne Alexander Vice-President, Education 212/605-6680	No
Amoco Corp. Amoco Foundation 200 E. Randolph Drive Chicago, IL 60601	Robert Arganbright Executive Director 312/856-6306	Yes
Andersen Foundation c/o Andersen Corporate 287 Central Ave. Bayport, MN 55003	Earl C. Swanson Vice-President 612/439-5150	No
Anheuser Busch Co., Inc. Anheuser-Busch Charitable Trust One Busch Place St. Louis, MO 63118	Nancy Calcaterra Contributors Administration 314/577-2454	No
Ashland Oil, Inc. Ashland Oil Foundation P.O. Box 391 Ashland, KY 41114	Judy B. Thomas President 606/329-4525	Yes
ARCO Foundation 515 S. Flower Street Los Angeles, CA 90071	Eugene R. Wilson President 213/486-3342	Yes
BankAmerica Corp. BankAmerica Foundation Box 37000, Dept. 3246 San Francisco, CA 94137	Caroline Boitano Vice-President, Senior Program Officer 415/953-0927	Yes
Bat Hanadiv Foundation c/o Carter, Ledyard & Milburn 2 Wall Street New York, NY 10005	Jerome Caulfield Attorney	No
Beatrice (BCI Holdings) E-11 Foundation Two N. LaSalle Street Chicago, IL 60602	Mariita Conley Executive Director 312/558-3758	No
Bell Atlantic Corp. 1310 N. Courthouse Road Arlington, VA 22201	Ruth Caine Director, Corporate Contributions 703/974-8814	No

Bell South Corp. Bell South Foundation 1155 Peach Tree Street, NE Atlanta, GA 30367	Leslie Graitcer Executive Director 404/420-8896	No
Benedum Foundation 1400 Benedum-Trees Building Pittsburgh, PA 15222	Beverly R. Walters Director, Grants Program 412/288-0360	No
Charles K. Blandin Foundation 10 Pokegama Avenue, N. Grand Rapids, MN 55744	Paul M. Olson President 218/326-0523	Yes
The Boeing Company P.O. Box 3707 M/S 18-83 Seattle, WA 98111	Joe A. Taller, Director Carver Gayton, Manager Educational Relations and Training 206/655-6679	Yes
BP America (Standard Oil) 200 Public Square 35-A Cleveland, OH 44114	Lance C. Buhl Manager, Corporate Contributions 216/586-8625	Yes
Lynde and Harry Bradley Foundation 777 E. Wisconsin Avenue Milwaukee, WI 53202	Michael S. Joyce Executive Director 414/291-9915	Yes
The Brown Foundation P.O. Box 13646 Houston, TX 77219	Katherine B. Dobelman Executive Director 713/523-6867	Yes
Burlington Northern, Inc. Burlington Northern Foundation 999 Third Avenue Seattle, WA 98109	Donald K. North President 206/467-3895	Yes
Fritz B. Burns Foundation 4001 W. Alameda Avenue Burbank, CA 91505	Joseph E. Rawlinson President 818/840-8802	Yes
The Bush Foundation East 900 First National Bank Building St. Paul, MN 55101	Humphrey Doermann President 612/227-0891	Yes
Callaway Foundation 209 Broome Street P.O. Box 790 LaGrange, GA 30241	J. T. Gresham General Manager 404/884-7348	Yes

Morris & Gwendolyn Cafritz Foundation 1825 K Street, N.W. Washington, DC 20006	Eugene E. Hines Administrative Assistant 202/862-6800	No
Carnegie Corp. of New York 437 Madison Avenue New York, NY 10022	Dorothy Knapp Secretary 212/371-3200	Yes
Amon G. Carter Foundation 1212 Interfirst Bank Building P.O. Box 1036 Ft. Worth, TX 76101	Bob J. Crow Executive Director 817/332-2783	Yes
Anne E. Casey Foundation 31 Brookside Drive Greenwich, CT 06830	Martin Schwartz Executive Directorr 203/661-2773	No
Caterpillar, Inc. Caterpillar Foundation 100 N.E. Adams Street Peoria, IL 61629	Edward W. Siebert Manager, Corporate Support Programs 309/675-5080	No
Chase Manhattan Corp. Chase Manhattan Foundation 44 Wall Street New York, NY 10081	David Ford Director, Philanthropic Activities 212/676-5080	Yes
Chevron USA, Inc. P.O. Box 7753 San Francisco, CA 94120	J. W. Rhodes, Jr. Manager, Contributions 415/894-5464	Yes
Chrysler Corp. Chrysler Corp. Fund P.O. Box 1919 Detroit, MI 48288	Lynn A. Feldhouse Administrator 313/956-5194	No
CIGNA Corporation CIGNA Foundation One Logan Square Philadelphia, PA 19103	Jeffrey P. Lindtner Executive Director 215/523-5255	No
Citicorp USA 200 S. Wacker Drive Chicago, IL 60606	Elizabeth Howland Vice-President 312/993-3000	Yes
Edna McConnell Clark Foundation 250 Park Avenue New York, NY 10017	Peter D. Bell President 212/986-7050	Yes

The Coastal Corporation Coastal Tower Nine Greenway Plaza Houston, TX 77046	Truman Arnold Vice-President, Administrative Services 713/877-1400	No
The Coca Cola Company Coca Cola Foundation P.O. Drawer 1734 Atlanta, GA 30301	Margaret J. Cox Vice-President, Executive Director, Foundation 404/676-2568	No
Commonwealth Fund One E. 75th Street New York, NY 10021-2692	Cynthia Woodcock Assistant Vice-President, Program Finance and Management 212/535-0400	No
CSX P.O. Box C-32222 Richmond, VA 23219	Raymond P. Szabo Assistant Vice-President, Corporate Services 804/782-1439	No
Charles A. Dana Foundation 150 E. 52nd Street New York, NY 10022	M. Baldwin Program Officer 212/223-4040	No
The Danforth Foundation 231 S. Bemiston Avenue St. Louis, MO 63105	Gene L. Schwilck President 314/862-6200	No
Dayton Hudson Corp. Dayton Hudson Foundation 777 Nicollet Mall Minneapolis, MN 55402	Cynthia Mayeda Managing Director 612/370-6555	No
Arthur S. DeMoss Foundation St. Davids Center St. Davids, PA 19087	Mrs. Arthur DeMoss Chief Executive Officer 215/254-5500	No
Digital Equipment Corporation 111 Powdermill Road MSO/K1 Maynard, MA 01754	Lee Richardson Manager, Education 617/493-2221	Yes
Dow Chemical USA Dow Chemical Co., Foundation P.O. Box 1751 Midland, MI 48674	Cherie A. Hutter Program Manager 517/636-1162	No
Duke Endowment 200 S. Tryon Street Charlotte, NC 28202	John F. Day Executive Director 704/376-0291	No

E. I. Dupont DeNemours
Dupont Company
9067 Dupont Building
Wilmington, DE 19898
	John T. Lund
	Executive Director,
	  Committee on Education
	  Aid
	302/774-5025
		Yes

Eastman Kodak Company
  Charitable Trust
343 State Street
Rochester, NY 14650
	Stanley C. Wright
	Director, Corporate
	  Contributions
	716/724-3127
		Yes

Exxon Education Foundation 180 Park Avenue P.O. Box 101 Florham Park, NJ 07932	Arnold R. Shore Executive Director 201/765-3004	Yes
Sherman Fairchild Foundation 71 Arch Street Greenwich, CT 06830	Patricia A. Lydan Vice-President 203/661-9360	Yes

Federal National Mortgage
  Association
3900 Wisconsin Avenue, N.W.
Washington, DC 20016
	Harriet Izey
	Vice-President, Community
	  Relations
	202/537-7000
		No

Federated Department Stores Federated Department Stores Foundation 7 W. Seventh Street Cincinnati, OH 45202	Thomas G. Cody Senior Vice-President 513/579-7068	No
Fleming Companies, Inc. 6301 Waterford Boulevard Box 26647 Oklahoma City, OK 73126	Cheryl Hodak Director, Corporate Communications 405/840-7200	No
The Ford Foundation 320 E. 43rd Street New York, NY 10017	Barron M. Tenny Secretary 212/573-5000	Yes
Ford Motor Company Ford Motor Co. Fund The American Road Dearborn, MI 48121	Leo J. Brennan, Jr. Executive Director, Foundation 313/845-8711	Yes
Gannett Foundation Lincoln Tower Rochester, NY 14604	Eugene C. Dorsey President 716/262-3315	Yes
GAR Foundation 50 S. Main Street Akron, OH 44309	Lisle M. Buckingham Trustee 216/376-5300	Yes

General Dynamics Corp. Material Service Corp. 222 N. LaSalle Street Chicago, IL 60601	Louis Levy Administrative Vice-President 312/372-3600	Yes
General Electric Co. General Electric Foundation 3135 Eastern Turnpike Fairfield, CT 06431	Paul M. Ostergard President 203/373-3216	Yes
General Motors Corp. General Motors Foundation 3044 W. Grand Boulevard Detroit, MI 48202	Ralph Frederick Director, Placement and College Relations 313/556-4260	Yes
Georgia-Pacific Co. Georgia Pacific Foundation 133 Peachtree Street, N.E. Atlanta, GA 30303	Wayne Tamblyn Treasurer 404/521-5228	No
The Getty Grant Program 401 Wilshire Boulevard Santa Monica, CA 90401	Gwen I. Walden Program Assistant 213/393-4244	Yes
Horace W. Goldsmith Foundation c/o Paskus, Gordon, Hyman 45 Rockefeller Plaza New York, NY 10111	Robert R. Slaughter Chief Executive 212/206-4113	Yes

Goodyear Tire & Rubber Co.
Goodyear Tire & Rubber
   Co. Fund
1144 E. Market Street
Akron, OH 44316
	Patricia A. Kemph
	Assistant Secretary,
	   Foundation
	216/796-2916
		No

The Great Atlantic & Pacific Tea Co., Inc. 2 Paragon Drive Montvale, NJ 07645	William Vitulli 201/573-9700	No
GTE Corp. GTE Foundation One Stamford Forum Stamford, CT 06904	Jorge Jackson Director, Corporate Social Responsibility 203/965-3620	No
George Gund Foundation One Erieview Plaza Cleveland, OH 44114	Henry C. Doll Acting Director 216/241-3114	Yes
Hall Family Foundations Charitable Investments P.O. Box 580 Kansas City, MO 64141	Margaret H. Pence Program Affairs 816/274-5615	Yes

John A. Hartford Foundation 55 E. 59th Street New York, NY 10022	Steven C. Eyre Executive Director 212/832-7788	No
William Randolph Hearst Foundation 888 Seventh Avenue New York, NY 10106	Robert M. Frehse, Jr. Executive Director 212/586-5404	No
Howard Heinz Endowment 301 Fifth Avenue Pittsburgh, PA 15222	Alfred W. Wishart, Jr. Executive Director 412/391-5122	Yes
Herrick Foundation 2500 Comerica Building Detroit, MI 48226	Kenneth G. Herrick President 313/963-6420	Yes
William and Flora Hewlett Foundation 525 Middlefield Road Menlo Park, CA 94025	Roger W. Heyns President 415/329-1070	No
Hewlett-Packard Company 3000 Hanover Street Palo Alto, CA 94304	Roderick Carlson Director of Corporate Grants 415/857-3053	No
Conrad N. Hilton Foundation 10100 Santa Monica Boulevard Los Angeles, CA 90067	Donald H. Hubbs President 213/556-4694	No
Honeywell Honeywell Foundation Honeywell Plaza Minneapolis, MN 55408	M. Patricia Hoven Director, Foundation 612/870-6821	Yes
Houston Endowment, Inc. P.O. Box 52338 Houston, TX 77052	J. H. Creekmore President 713/223-4043	Yes
IBM Corporation 500 Columbus Avenue Thornwood, NY 10594	Dr. John C. Porter Director, University Relations 914/742-5800	Yes
The James Irwin Foundation One Market Plaza Stevart Street Tower San Francisco, CA 94104	Liz A. Vega Director, Grants Program 415/777-2244	No
ITI Corporation 320 Park Avenue New York, NY 10022	Joseph Santangelo Director, Public Affairs 212/752-6000	No

Robert Wood Johnson Foundation P.O. Box 2316 Princeton, NJ 08543	Edward H. Robbins Proposal Manager 609/452-8701	Yes
Johnson & Johnson Co. Johnson & Johnson Family of Companies Contribution Foundation One Johnson & Johnson Plaza New Brunswick, NJ 08543	Herbert T. Nelson Vice-President 201/524-6747	Yes
W. Alton Jones Foundation 433 Park Street Charlottesville, VA 22901	Richard D. Johnson Director 804/295-2134	Yes
Joyce Foundation 135 S. LaSalle Street Chicago, IL 60603	Craig Kennedy President 312/782-2464	Yes
The Henry J. Kaiser Family Foundation 2400 Sand Hill Road Menlo Park, CA 94025	Barbara H. Kehrer Vice-President 415/854-9400	No
W. K. Kellogg Foundation 400 North Avenue Battle Creek, MI 49017	Norman A. Brown President 616/968-1611	Yes
Peter Kiewit Foundation Woodmen Tower Farnam at Seventeenth Omaha, NE 68102	Lyn Wallin Ziegenbein Executive Director 402/344-7890	No
F. M. Kirby Foundation 17 DeHart Street Morristown, NJ 07960	Fred M. Kirby II President 201/538-4800	Yes
K-Mart Corp. Public Affairs 3100 W. Big Beaver Road Troy, MI 48084	James Chrilla Vice-President/Treasurer 313/643-1000	No
Knight Foundation One Cascade Plaza Akron, OH 44308	Creed C. Black President 216/253-9301	Yes
Kraft Inc. Kraft Foundation Kraft Court Glenview, IL 60025	Ronald Coman Administrative Director 312/998-7032	Yes

Kresge Foundation P.O. Box 3151 3215 W. Big Beaver Road Troy, MI 48007	Alfred H. Taylor, Jr. President 313/643-9630	No
Kroger Co. 1014 Vine Street Cincinnati, OH 45201	James D. McIntire Vice-President/Secretary 513/762-1149	No
Lilly Endowment 2801 N. Meridian Street P.O. Box 88068 Indianapolis, IN 46208	James T. Morris President 317/924-5471	No
Loews Corp. Loews Foundation 666 Fifth Avenue New York, NY 10103	C. G. Sposato, Jr. Trustee 212/545-2000	No
Longwood Foundation 1004 Wilmington Trust Center Wilmington, DE 19801	Endsley P. Fairman Executive Secretary 302/654-2477	No
Henry Luce Foundation 111 W. 50th Street New York, NY 10020	Robert E. Armstrong Executive Director 212/489-7700	No
Lucky Stores, Inc. 6300 Clark Avenue Dublin, CA 94568	Janice Vance Secretary, Contribution Program 415/833-6000	No
J.E. & L.E. Mabee Foundation 3000 Mid-Continent Tower Tulsa, OK 74103	Guy R. Mabee Director 918/584-4286	No
John & Catherine MacArthur Foundation 140 S. Dearborn Street Chicago, IL 60603	James M. Furman Executive Vice-President 312/726-8000	Yes
Robert R. McCormick Charitable Trust 435 N. Michigan Avenue Chicago, IL 60611	Claude A. Smith Executive Vice-President 312/222-3512	Yes
McCune Foundation 1104 Commonwealth Building 316 Fourth Avenue Pittsburgh, PA 15222	Earland I. Carlson Executive Director 412/644-8779	No

McDonnell Douglas Corp. McDonnell Douglas Foundation P.O. Box 516 St. Louis, MO 63166	Walter Diggs Corporate Secretary, Charitable Affairs 314/232-8464	No
The McKnight Foundation 410 Peavey Building Minneapolis, MN 55402	Russell V. Ewald Executive Vice-President 612/333-4220	No
Manufacturers Hanover Corp. Manufacturers Hanover Foundation 270 Park Avenue New York, NY 10017	Matthew Trachtenberg Agent-Foundation 212/286-7118	No
Meadows Foundation Wilson Historic Block 2922 Swiss Avenue Dallas, TX 75204	Sally R. Lancaster Executive Vice-President 214/826-9431	Yes
Andrew W. Mellon Foundation 140 E. 62nd Street New York, NY 10021	J. Kellum Smith, Jr. Vice-President 212/838-8400	No
Richard King Mellon Foundation 525 William Penn Place Pittsburgh, PA 15219	George H. Taber Vice-President 412/392-2800	Yes
Merrill Lynch & Co. Merrill Lynch & Co. Foundation One Liberty Plaza 165 Broadway New York, NY 10080	Westina Matthews Secretary, Foundation 212/236-4319	No
Fred Meyer Charitable Trust 1515 S.W. Fifth Avenue Portland, OR 97201	Charles S. Rooks Executive Director 503/228-5512	Yes
Minnesota Mining & Manufacturing Foundation Building 521-11-01 3M Center St. Paul, MN 55144	Eugene W. Steele Manager, Contributions Program 612/736-3781	Yes
Mobil Oil Corp. Mobil Foundation, Inc. 150 E. 42nd Street New York, NY 10017	Richard G. Mund Secretary, Executive Director 212/883-2174	No

Monsanto Co. Monsanto Fund 800 N. Lindbergh Boulevard St. Louis, MO 63167	Dr. John L. Masom President 314/694-4596	Yes
Moody Foundation 704 Moody National Bank Building Galveston, TX 77550	Roberta Ruocco Vice-President 212/483-2058	Yes

Morgan Guaranty Trust Co.
  of New York
Morgan Guaranty Trust Co.
  Charitable Fund
23 Wall Street
New York, NY 10015
	Peter M. Moore
	Grants Officer
	409/763-5333
		Yes

Charles Stewart Mott
  Foundation
1200 Mott Foundation
  Building
Flint, MI 48502
	Frank Gilsdorf
	Vice-President
	313/238-5651
		Yes

M. J. Murdock Charitable Trust 703 Broadway Vancouver, WA 98660	Sam C. Smith Executive Director 206/694-8415	No
Mabel Pew Myrin Trust Three Parkway Philadelphia, PA 19102	Fred H. Billups, Jr. Executive Director 215/568-3330	No
Samuel Roberts Noble Foundation P.O. Box 2180 Ardmore, OK 73402	John F. Snodgrass President 405/223-5810	Yes
Northwest Area Foundation W. 975 First National Bank Building St. Paul, MN 55101	Terry Tinson Saario President 612/224-9635	No
Nynex, Inc. 500 Westchester Avenue White Plains, NY 10604	Patricia Fogarty 914/683-1096	No

Occidental Petroleum
Occidental Petroleum
  Charitable Foundation,
  Inc.
10889 Wilshire Boulevard
Los Angeles, CA 90024
	Evelyn S. Wong
	Assistant Secretary, Treasurer
	213/879-1700
		Yes

F. W. Olin Foundation 805 Third Avenue New York, NY 10022	Lawrence W. Milas President 212/832-0508	No
Pacific Gas & Electric Co. 77 Beale Street San Francisco, CA 94106	Patricia Prado Contributions Programs 415/973-4951	No
Pacific Telesis Group Pacific Telesis Foundation 130 Kearny Street, Room 3309 San Francisco, CA 94108	Mary E. Leslie Executive Director, Education 415/394-3683	Yes
David & Lucille Packard Foundation 300 Second Street Los Altos, CA 94022	Colburn S. Wilbur Executive Director 415/948-7658	Yes
William Penn Foundation 1630 Locust Street Philadelphia, PA 19103	Dr. Bernard C. Watson President 215/732-5114	Yes
J. C. Penney Co. P.O. Box 659000 Dallas, TX 75265	Robin Morrison Manager, Corporate Contributions 214/591-1966	Yes
PepsiCo-Inc. PepsiCo Foundation 700 Anderson Hill Road Purchase, NY 10577	Jacqueline R. Millan Manager, Corporate Contributions 914/253-3908	Yes
J. Howard Pew Freedom Trust Three Parkway Philadelphia, PA 19102	Fred H. Billups, Jr. Executive Director 215/568-3330	Yes
J. N. Pew, Jr. Charitable Trust Three Parkway Philadelphia, PA 19102	Fred H. Billups, Jr. Executive Director 215/568-3330	Yes
Pew Memorial Trust Three Parkway Philadelphia, PA 19102	Fred H. Billups, Jr. Executive Director 215/568-3330	Yes
Phillips Petroleum Cos. 120 Park Avenue New York, NY 10017	Annette T. D'Annunizo Secretary, Corporate Support Program 212/880-3366	Yes

El Pomar Foundation P.O. Box 158 Colorado Springs, CO 80901	William J. Hybl President 303/633-7733	Yes
The Procter & Gamble Co. Procter & Gamble Fund P.O. Box 599 Cincinnati, OH 45202	Bernard J. Nolan Vice-President, Secretary 513/562-2201	Yes
Public Welfare Foundation 2600 Virginia Avenue, N.W. Washington, DC 20037	Charles Glenn Ihrig Executive Director 202/965-1800	Yes
Raytheon Co. Raytheon Charitable Foundation 141 Spring Street Lexington, MA 02173	Janet C. Taylor Corporate Contributions Manager 617/862-6600	Yes
Kate B. Reynolds Charitable Trust Eight W. Third Street Winston-Salem, NC 27101	W. Vance Frye Executive Secretary 919/723-1456	Yes
H. Smith Richardson Charitable Trust P.O. Box 20124 Greensboro, NC 27420	Dorothy W. Hurley Administrative Vice-President 919/379-8600	No
RJR Nabisco, Inc. P.O. Box 2959 Winston-Salem, NC 27150	John Bacon Director, Corporate Contributions 919/741-5377	No
Rockefeller Brothers Fund 1290 Avenue of the Americas New York, NY 10104	Benjamin R. Shute, Jr. Secretary 212/373-4200	Yes
Rockefeller Foundation 1133 Avenue of the Americas New York, NY 10036	Lynda Mullen Secretary 212/869-8500	Yes
Rockwell International Corp. Rockwell International Corp. Trust 600 Grant Street Pittsburgh, PA 15219	J. J. Christin Secretary 412/565-5803	Yes
Safeway Stores, Inc. Fourth and Jackson Streets Oakland, CA 94660	Felicia M. delCampo Manager, Public Affairs 415/598-3267	No

Santa Fe Southern Pacific Corp. Santa Fe Southern Pacific Foundation 224 Michigan Avenue Chicago, IL 60604	R. L. Holden Executive Director, Foundation 312/786-6204	No
Sara Lee Corp. Sara Lee Foundation 3 First National Plaza Chicago, IL 60602	Gretchen Miller-Reimel Manager, Corporate Contributions 312/558-8458	No
Sarah Scaife Foundation P.O. Box 268 Pittsburgh, PA 15230	Richard M. Larry President 412/392-2900	Yes
Sears, Roebuck Co. Sears-Roebuck Foundation Dept. 903 BSC51-02 Chicago, IL 60684	Paula A. Banks Vice-President, Executive Director 312/875-8337	Yes
Norton Simon Art Foundation 411 W. Colorado Boulevard Pasadena, CA 91105	Walter W. Timoshuk Vice-President 818/449-6840	Maybe
Norton Simon Foundation 411 W. Colorado Boulevard Pasadena, CA 91105	Walter W. Timoshuk Vice-President 818/449-6840	No
The Skillman Foundation 333 W. Fort Street Detroit, MI 48226	Kari Schlachtenhaufen Program Officer 313/961-8853	Yes
Alfred P. Sloan Foundation 630 Fifth Avenue New York, NY 10111	Albert Rees President 212/582-0450	Yes
The Southern Co. P.O. Box 1151 Pensacola, FL 32520	Janette Skaggs Secretary, Gulf Power Co. 904/444-5111	Yes
The Southland Corp. Southland Foundation 5215 N. O'Connor Boulevard Irving, TX 75039	J. Michael Lewis Secretary, Foundation 214/556-0500	No
Southwestern Bell Corp. Southwestern Bell Foundation One Bell Center St. Louis, MO 63101	Charles O. DeReimer Executive Director, Foundation 314/235-7040	No

Spencer Foundation 875 N. Michigan Avenue Chicago, IL 60611	Marion M. Faldet Vice-President 312/337-7000	Yes
Starr Foundation 70 Pine Street New York, NY 10270	Ta Chun Hsu President 212/770-6882	Yes
The Stratford Foundation One Federal Street Boston, MA 02211	Peter A. Wilson Director 617/292-3885	Yes
Sun Co. 100 Matsonford Road Radnor, PA 19087	Dolores A. Kellenbenz Administrator, Social Investment 215/293-6555	No
Super Value Stores P.O. Box 990 Minneapolis, MN 55440	John Seltzer Chairman 612/828-4000	Yes
Surdna Foundation 250 Park Avenue New York, NY 10177	M. Lindsley Homrighausen Administrator for Grants 212/697-0630	No
Anne B. & Charles B. Tandy Foundation 1577 Inter First Tower 801 Cherry Street Fort Worth, TX 76102	Thomas F. Beech Executive Vice-President 817/877-3344	Yes
Tenneco, Inc. Box 2511 Houston, TX 76102	JoAnn Swinney Director, Community Affairs 713/757-3930	Yes
Texaco, Inc. Texaco Philanthropic Foundation 2000 Westchester Avenue White Plains, NY 10650	Maria Mike-Mayer Secretary, Foundation 914/253-4150	No
T.L.L. Temple Foundation 109 Temple Boulevard Lufkin, TX 75901	Ward R. Burke Executive Secretary 409/639-5197	Yes
Travelers Corp. The Travelers Cos. Foundation, Inc. One Tower Square Hartford, CT 06183	Ernest L. Osborne President 203/277-4079	No
Union Carbide Corp. 39 Old Ridgebury Road Danbury, CT 06817	Clyde Greenert Director, Contributions 203/794-2000	No

Union Pacific Corp. Union Pacific Foundation 345 Park Avenue New York, NY 10154	Heather Hollowell Manager 212/418-7926	No
United Technologies Corp. One Financial Plaza Hartford, CT 06101	Richard Cole Manager, Corporation Contributions 203/728-7943	Yes
Unocal Unocal Foundation 1201 W. 5th Street Los Angeles, CA 90017	R. P. Van Zandt Vice-President 213/977-6172	No
US West, Inc. 7800 E. Orchard Road Inglewood, CA 90111	Judy Servoff, Vice-President Jane J. Prancan, Director Corporate Community Relations 303/793-6500	No
USX Corp. USX Foundation 600 Grant Street Pittsburgh, PA 15230	William A. Gregory, Jr. Manager, Foundation 412/433-5237	No
DeWitt Wallace Fund 1270 Avenue of the Americas New York, NY 10020	Arlene Shuler Deputy Director 212/489-1540	Yes
Wal-Mart Stores, Inc. Wal-Mart Foundation 702 S.W. Eighth Street Bentonville, AK 72716	James Von Gremp Director, Foundation 501/273-4000	No
William K. Warren Foundation P.O. Box 470372 Tulsa, OK 74147	W. R. Lissau President 918/492-8100	No
Robert A. Welch Foundation 4605 Post Oak Place Houston, TX 77027	Norbert Dittrich Executive Manager 713/961-9884	No
Westinghouse Electric Corp. Westinghouse Educational Foundation Westinghouse Building Gateway Center Pittsburgh, PA 15222	Cecile Springer President 412/642-6035	No
Whitaker Foundation 875 Poplar Church Road Camp Hill, PA 17011	Miles J. Gibbons, Jr. Executive Director 717/763-1391	No

Joseph B. Whitehead Foundation 1400 Peachtree Center Tower 230 Peach Tree Street, N.W. Atlanta, GA 30303	Boisfeuillet Jones, President Charles H. McTier, Vice-President 404/522-6755	Yes
Lettie Pate Whitehead Foundation 1400 Peachtree Center Tower 230 Peach Tree Street, N.W. Atlanta, GA 30303	Boisfeuillet Jones, President Charles H. McTier, Vice-President 404/522-6755	No
Wiengart Foundation 1200 Wilshire Boulevard Los Angeles, CA 90017	Charles W. Jacobson President 213/482-4343	No
Amherst Wilder Foundation 919 Lefond Avenue St. Paul, MN 55104	Leonard H. Wilkening President 612/642-4000	No
Winn-Dixie Stores Winn-Dixie Stores Foundation Box B Jacksonville, FL 32203	John Parker Jones President, Foundation 904/783-5000	No
Wortham Foundation 2777 Allen Parkway Houston, TX 77019	Allen H. Carruth President 713/526-8849	No
Xerox Corp. Xerox Foundation P.O. Box 1600 Stamford, CT 06904	Robert H. Gudger, Vice-President, Foundation Higher Education and Community Affairs	Yes

APPENDIX 2
Companies that Match to Junior or Community Colleges

The following is a list of corporations that match gifts of their employees to junior or community colleges:

ACF Industries, Inc.
AMP Incorporated
ARA Services, Inc.
AT&T
Abbott Laboratories
The Abell Foundation, Inc.
Adams Harkness & Hill, Inc.
The Aerospace Corporation
Aetna Life & Casualty
Aid Association for Lutherans
Air Products & Chemicals, Inc.
AKTion Associates, Inc.
Akzo America, Inc.
Albany International Corporation
Alberton's, Inc.
Alco Standard Corporation
Alexander & Baldwin, Inc.
Allegheny Ludlum Steel Corporation
Allendale Mutual Insurance Company
Allied-Signal Inc.
Allstate Insurance Companies
Alpha Industries, Inc.
Aluminum Company of America
AMAX, Inc.
Amcast Industrial Corporation
Amerada Hess Corporation
American Airlines, Inc.
American Broadcasting Companies, Inc.
American Brands, Inc.
American Cyanamid Company
American Electric Power Company, Inc.
American Express Company
American General Corporation
American Home Products Corporation
American International Group, Inc.
American Motors Corporation
American Medical International, Inc.
American Mutual Insurance Companies
American National Bank & Trust Company of Chicago
American Optical Corporation
American Sterilizer Company
American Standard, Inc.
American Stock Exchange
American States Insurance
American United Life Insurance Company
Ameritech Services, Inc.
AmeriTrust Company National Association
Amfac, Inc.
Amoco Corporation
Amstar Corporation
Arthur Andersen & Company
The Andersons
Anheuser-Busch Companies, Inc.
Appleton Papers, Inc.
Arkwright-Boston Manufacturers Mutual Insurance Company
Armco, Inc.
Arrow-Hart, Inc.
Ashland Oil, Inc.
Associated Box Corporation
Associated Dry Goods Corporation
Guy F. Atkinson Company of California
Atlantic Richfield Company
Automatic Data Processing, Inc.
AVCO Corporation
BASF Corporation
The BOC Group, Inc.
Badische Corporation
M. S. Bailey & Son, Bankers
Ball Corporation
Baltimore Bancorp
Bancroft-Whitney Company
Bank of Boston
The Bank of California, N.A.
Bank of New England, N.A.
The Bank of New York
Bank South
Bankers Life and Casualty
Bankers Trust Company
Barclays American Corporation
C. R. Bard, Inc.
Barnes Group, Inc.

Barnett Banks of Florida, Inc.
Barry Wright Corporation
The Barton-Gillet Company
BATUS Inc.
Baxter Travenol Labs, Inc.
BayBanks Inc.
Beatrice Companies, Inc.
Bechtel Power Corporation
A.G. Becker Paribas, Inc.
Becton Dickinson and Company
Beech Aircraft Corporation
Bell Communications Research, Inc.
Bell & Howell Company
Bell of Pennsylvania & Diamond State Telephone Company
BellSouth Corporation
Beloit Corporation
Benis Company, Inc.
The Bergen Record Corporation
Best Products Company
Bigelow-Sanford, Inc.
Bill Communications, Inc.
Bird Companies Charitable Foundation, Inc.
H & R Block, Inc.
Blount, Inc.
Blue Bell, Inc.
The Boeing Company
Boise Cascade Corporation
Borg-Warner Corporation
The Boston Globe Newspaper Company
Bowater Inc.
The Bowery Savings Bank
Bowes/Hanlon Advertising, Inc.
Brakeley, John Price Jones Inc.
Bernd Brecher and Associates, Inc.
Bristol-Myers Company
Brockway Glass Company, Inc.
Brown-Forman Corporation
John Brown Inc.
Brunswick Corporation
Buckbee Mears Company
Buell Industries, Inc.
Buffalo Color Corporation
Bunge Corporation
Burlington Industries, Inc.
Burlington Northern Inc.
Leo Burnett Company, Inc.
Burroughs Wellcome Company
Business Men's Assurance Company of America
Butler Manufacturing Company
CPC International Inc.
Cabot Corporation
Cabot's Stains
Calex Manufacturing Company, Inc.
Callanan Industries Inc.
Campbell Soup Company
Capital Cities/ABC, Inc.
Carolina Power & Light Company
Carolina Telephone & Telegraph Company
Carpenter Technology Corporation
Carson Pirie Scott & Company
Carter Hawley Hale Stores, Inc.
Carter-Wallace, Inc.
Castle and Cooke, Inc.
Celanese Corporation
Centel Corporation
Centerre Bank, N.A.
Central Illinois Light Company
Central Vermont Public Service Corporation
Century Companies of America
CertainTeed Corporation
Chamberlain Manufacturing Corporation
Champion International Corporation
The Chase Manhattan Corporation
Chemical Bank
Chemtech Industries, Inc.
Chesapeake Corporation
Chesapeake and Potomac Telephone Companies
Chesebrough-Pond's, Inc.
Chessie System Railroads
Chevron Corporation
Chicago Pneumatic Tool Company
Chigaco Title & Trust Company
Chicago Tribune Company
Chrysler Corporation
Chubb Life Insurance Company of America
Chubb & Son Inc.
Church Mutual Insurance Company
CIBA-Geigy Corporation
CIGNA Corporation
Cincinnati Bell, Inc.

Citicorp/Citibank
The Citizens and Southern Georgia Corporation
Citizens Fidelity Bank & Trust Company
The Cleveland-Cliffs Iron Company
Cleveland Electric Illuminating Company
The Clorox Company
The Coleman Company, Inc.
Colgate-Palmolive Company
Collins & Aikman Corporation
Colonial Bankcorp, Inc.
Colonial Penn Group, Inc.
Columbia Gas System, Inc.
The Columbus Mutual Life Insurance Company
Combustion Engineering, Inc.
Comerica Inc.
Commerical Union Insurance Companies
Commonwealth Energy System, Inc.
Commonwealth Insurance Company
Communications Satellite Corporation
Connecticut Savings Bank
Connecticut Bank & Trust Company
Connecticut Mutual Life Insurance Company
Connecticut Natural Gas Corporation
Conoco, Inc.
Consolidated Papers, Inc.
Consolidated Edison Company of New York, Inc.
Consolidation Coal Company
The Continental Corporation
Continental Telecom Inc.
Continental Can Company, Inc.
Co-Op Banking Group Companies
Cooper Industries
Cooper Tire & Rubber Company
The Copley Press, Inc.
Corning Glass Works
Cowles Media Company
Crane Company
Cray Research, Inc.
Criton Technologies
Crompton & Knowles Corporation
Cross & Trecker Corporation
Crum & Forster, Inc.
Cummins Engine Company, Inc.
Dain Bosworth Inc.
Dana Corporation
The Danforth Foundation
DEKALB Corporation
Delta Air Lines, Inc.
Delta U.S. Corporation
Deluxe Check Printers, Inc.
Dennison Manufacturing Company
Detroit Edison Company
A.W.G. Dewar Inc.
The Dexter Corporation
Diamond Crystal Salt Company
Diamond Shamrock Corporation
Difco Laboratories
Digital Equipment Corporation
Dillingham Corporation
Dominion Resources, Inc.
Donaldson Company Inc.
Donaldson, Lufkin & Jenrette
R. R. Donnelley & Sons Company
The Dow Chemical Company
Dow Corning Corporation
Dow Jones & Company, Inc.
Dry Dock Savings Bank
Duke Power Company
The Dun & Bradstreet Corporation
Durham Corporation
Duty Free Shoppers Group Ltd.
EG&G, Inc.
Eastern Gas and Fuel Associates
Eaton Corporation
Economics Laboratory, Inc.
Educators Mutual Life Insurance Company
Egan Machinery Company
Elf Aquitaine, Inc.
Emerson Electric Company
Emery Air Freight Corporation
Emhart Corporation
Englehard Corporation
Engineered Systems & Development Corporation
Enron Corporation
ENSERCH Corporation
Ensign-Bickford Foundation
Envirotech Corporation
Equibank
The Equitable Life Assurance Society of the U.S.

Equitable Life Insurance Company of Iowa
Ethicon, Inc.
Ethyl Corporation
European American Bank
Ex-Cell-O Corporation
Exxon Education Foundation
FMC Corporation
Facet Enterprises, Inc.
Factory Mutual Engineering & Research/Service Bureau
Fairchild Industries, Inc.
Farm Credit Banks of Springfield
Federal-Mogul Corporation
Federal National Mortgage Association
Federated Department Stores, Inc.
Ferro Corporation
Fiduciary Trust Company (Boston)
The Field Corporation
The Firestone Tire & Rubber Company
FirstBankcorp, Inc.
First Bank System, Inc.
The First Boston Corporation
First Chicago Corporation/The First National Bank of Chicago
First Hawaiian, Inc.
First Interstate Bank of California
First Kentucky National Corporation
First Maryland Bancorp
First Mississippi Corporation
First National Bank of Pennsylvania
First National Bank of Bartlesville, Oklahoma
The First National Bank of Atlanta
First Union Corporation
First Valley Bank (First Valley Corporation)
Fleet National Bank
Fluor Corporation
Ford Motor Company
The Foxboro Company
Freeport-McMoRan, Inc.
Fruehauf Corporation
H. B. Fuller Company
Funderburke & Associates, Inc.
GATX Corporation
GTE Corporation
E. & J. Gallo Winery
Gannett Foundation

Gary-Williams Oil Producer/The Piton Foundation
Gast Manufacturing Corporation
The Gates Corporation
GenCorp Inc.
General Accident Insurance Company of America
General Cable Company
General Cinema Corporation
General Defense Corporation
General Dynamics Corporation
General Electric Company
General Foods Corporation
General Housewares Corporation
General Mills, Inc.
General Signal Corporation
GenRad Foundation
Gilbane Building Company
Gilman Paper Company
P. H. Glatfelter Company
Glaxo, Inc.
Goldman, Sachs & Company
Goldome
The BF Goodrich Company
Gould, Inc.
Goulds Pumps, Inc.
W. R. Grace & Company
W. W. Grainger, Inc.
GrandMet USA, Inc.
The Graphic Printing Company Inc.
Great Lakes Carbon Corporation
Great Northern Nekoosa Corporation
Gregory Poole Equipment Company
Grinnell Mutual Reinsurance Company
Grumman Corporation
The Guardian Life Insurance Company of America
Gulf & Western Inc.
Hackney Industries Inc.
Halliburton Company
Hallmark Cards, Inc.
Hamilton Bank
Hampton & Harper, Inc.
M. A. Hanna Company
Harper & Row Publishers, Inc.
Harris Bank
Harris Corporation
Harsco Corporation
Hartford National Corporation

The Hartford Steam Boiler
  Inspection and Insurance
  Company
H. J. Heinz Company
Hercules Inc.
Hershey Entertainment & Resort
  Company
Hershey Foods Corporation
Hewitt Associates
The Higbee Company
Higher Education Publications
Hoffman-LaRoche Inc.
Holiday Corporation
Holmes & Narver, Inc.
Homestake Mining Company
Geo. A. Hormel & Company
Hospital Corporation of America
Houghton Mifflin Company
Household International, Inc.
Harvey Hubbell, Inc.
J. M. Huber Corporation
Huck Manufacturing Company
Huffy Corporation
Hughes Aircraft Company
E. F. Hutton & Company, Inc.
The Hydraulic Company
IC Industries, Inc.
ICI Americas Inc.
IDS Financial Services Inc.
ITT Corporation
IU International
Illinois Bell
Illinois Tool Works Inc.
Indiana Bell Telephone Company,
  Inc.
Industrial Indemnity Company
Industrial Risk Insurers
Ingersoll-Rand Company
Instron Corporation
Integon Corporation
Intel Corporation
Intelligent Controls, Inc.
The Interlake Corporation
International Flavors and Fragrances
  Inc.
International Multifoods
  Corporation
International Paper Company
International Minerals & Chemical
  Corporation
International Business Machines
  Corporation

Iowa Resource Inc.
Itek Corporation
JSJ Corporation
Jack Eckerd Corporation
James River Corporation
Jamesbury Corporation
Jefferies & Company, Inc.
Jefferson-Pilot Communications
  Company
Jefferson-Pilot Corporation
Jewel Companies, Inc.
John Hancock Mutual Life
  Insurance Company
A. Johnson & Company, Inc.
Johnson Controls, Inc.
Johnson & Higgins
Johnson & Johnson
S. C. Johnson & Son, Inc.
Jones Group, Inc.
Jostens, Inc.
K Mart Corporation
Kansas City Southern Industries,
  Inc.
Keebler Company
Keefe, Bruyette & Woods, Inc.
Kellogg Company
The M. W. Kellogg Company
Kellogg Group
The Kerite Company
Kerr-McGee Corporation
Kidder, Peabody & Company, Inc.
Kingsbury Machine Tool
  Corporation
Kiplinger Washington Editors
Knight-Ridder Newspapers, Inc.
H. Kornstamm & Company, Inc.
Koppers Company, Inc.
Kraft, Inc.
Lanier Business Products, Inc., A
  Harris Company
LaSalle National Bank
The Law Company, Inc.
The Lawyers Co-operative
  Publishing Company
Lehigh Portland Cement Company
Lever Brothers Company
Levi Strauss & Company
The Liberty Corporation
Eli Lilly and Company
Lincoln National Corporation
Thomas J. Lipton, Inc.
Little, Brown and Company

Loews Corporation
Lone Star Industries, Inc.
Lotus Development Corporation
The Louisiana Land and
 Exploration Company
Lubrizol Corporation
Lucky Stores, Inc.
Ludlow Corporation
Lukens Inc.
Lummus Crest, Inc.
Lutheran Brotherhood
MCA Inc.
MSI Insurance
M & T Chemicals Incorporated
MTS Systems Corporation
John D. and Catherine T.
 MacArthur Foundation
Mack Trucks, Inc.
R. H. Macy & Company, Inc.
Maguire Oil Company
Manufacturers Hanover Corporation
Manufacturers National Corporation
Marathon Oil Company
Maremont Corporation
The Marine Corporation
Marine Midland Bank, N.A.
Maritz Inc.
Mark Controls Corporation
Marsh & McLennan Companies, Inc.
Martin Marietta Corporation
Massachusetts Mutual Life Insurance
 Company
Mast Drug Company
Mattel, Inc.
The May Department Stores
 Company
McCormick & Company, Inc.
McDonald's Corporation
McDonnell Douglas Corporation
McGraw-Hill, Inc.
McKesson Corporation
McQuay, Inc.
The Mead Corporation
Mebane Packaging Corporation
Mechanics Bank
Medtronic, Inc.
Mellon Bank Corporation
Merck & Company, Inc.
Meredith Corporation
Merit Oil Corporation
Meritor Financial Group
Merrill Lynch & Company, Inc.

Metropolitan Life Insurance
 Company
Mettler Instrument Corporation
Michigan Bell Telephone Company
Middlesex Mutual Assurance
 Company
The Midland Mutual Life Insurance
 Company
Midland-Ross Corporation
Midatlantic Banks Inc.
Miehle-Goss-Dexter Inc.
Milliken & Company
Millipore Corporation
Milton Bradley Company
Minnesota Mining & Manufacturing
 Company, Inc.
Minnesota Mutual Life Insurance
 Company
The Mitre Corporation
Mobil Oil Corporation
Mohasco Corporation
Monarch Capital Company
Monsanto Company
The Montana Power Company
Montgomery Ward & Company,
 Inc.
Monumental Corporation
MONY Financial Services
MOOG Incorporated
Moore Financial Group, Inc.
Moore McCormack Resources, Inc.
Morgan Construction Company
Morgan Guaranty Trust Company
 of New York
Morgan Stanley & Company,
 Incorporated
Morrison-Knudsen Company, Inc.
Morse Shoe, Inc.
Motorola Inc.
Charles Stewart Mott Foundation
Murphy Oil USA, Inc.
Mutual of America
Mutual Benefit Life
Mutual of Omaha
NACCO Industries, Inc.
NCNB Corporation
NCR Corporation
NL Industries, Inc.
NRC, Inc.
Nabisco Brands, Inc.
Nalco Chemical Company
National City Corporation

National Can Corporation
National Distillers and Chemical
   Corporation
National Gypsum Company
National Life Insurance Company
National Medical Enterprises, Inc.
National Steel Corporation
National Westminster Bank USA
Nationwide Mutual Insurance
   Company
Nepera, Inc.
The New England Education Loan
   Marketing Corporation
New England Business Service, Inc.
New England Electric System
   Companies
New England Telephone
New Jersey Bell Telephone Company
New Jersey Natural Gas Company
The New York Bank for Savings
New York Life Insurance Company
New York Telephone
The New York Times Company
The New Yorker Magazine Inc.
Newsweek, Inc.
The Samuel Roberts Nobel
   Foundation, Inc.
Nordson Corporation
Norfolk Southern Corporation
North American Philips Corporation
Northeast Utilities
Northern Illinois Gas
Northern States Power Company
The Northern Trust Company
Northern Telecom, Inc.
Northwest Airlines, Inc.
Northwest Industries, Inc.
Northwestern National Life
   Insurance Company
Northwestern Bell Corporation
Northwestern Mutual Life Insurance
   Company
Norton Company
W. W. Norton & Company, Inc.
Northwest Corporation
Noxell Corporation
John Nuveen & Company
   Incorporated
NYNEX Corporation
Occidental Oil & Gas Company
Occidental Petroleum Corporation
Ohio Bell Telephone Company

Ohio Edison Company
The Ohio National Life Insurance
   Company
Oklahoma Gas and Electric
   Company
Old Stone Bank
Olin Corporation
Oneida Ltd.
Oregon Portland Cement Company
Owens-Corning Fiberglass
   Corporation
Owens-Illinois, Inc.
Oxford Industries, Inc.
PHH Group, Inc.
PPG Industries, Inc.
PQ Corporation
Paccar, Inc.
Pacific Lighting Corporation
Pacific Mutual Life Insurance
   Company
Pacific Northwest Bell Telephone
   Company
Pacific Resources, Inc.
Panhandle Eastern Corporation
Parker-Hannifin Corporation
The Paul Revere Companies
Pearle Health Services, Inc.
Pechiney Corporation
Penn Central Telecommunications
   Company
The Penn Central Corporation
J. C. Penney Company, Inc.
Pennsylvania Power & Light
   Company
Pennwalt Corporation
Pennzoil Company
People's Bank
The People's Gas Light and Coke
   Company
PepsiCo.-Inc.
PET Incorporated
Pfizer, Inc.
Phelps Dodge Corporation
Philadelphia National Bank
Philip Morris Companies, Inc.
Phillips Petroleum Company
Phoenix Mutual Life Insurance
   Company
Piedmont Aviation, Inc.
The Pillsbury Company
The Pioneer Group, Inc.
Pioneer Hi-Bred International, Inc.

Piper, Jaffray & Hopwood Inc.
Pitney Bowes, Inc.
Pittsburgh National Bank
Pittway Corporation
Plante & Moran, CPA's
Playboy Enterprises, Inc.
Pneumo Abex Corporation
Pogo Producing Company
Polaroid Corporation
Pope & Talbot, Inc.
Potlatch Corporation
Preformed Line Products Company
Premark International, Inc.
Price Brothers Company
T. Rowe Price Associates, Inc.
Primerica Corporation
The Principal Financial Group
The Prospect Hill Foundation
Protection Mutual Insurance Company
Provident Life and Accident Insurance Company
Provident Mutual Life Insurance Company
Provident National Bank
The Prudential Insurance Company of America
Public Service Company of Colorado
Public Service Electric and Gas Company
Puget Sound Power & Light Company
Quaker Chemical Corporation
The Quaker Oats Company
Quaker State Oil Refining Corporation
R.J.R. Nabisco, Inc.
RKO General, Inc.
Rainier Bancorporation
Arthur D. Raybin Associates, Inc.
Raytheon Company
Reader's Digest Association, Inc.
Reading & Bates Corporation
Reliance Electric Company
Reliance Insurance Companies
Republic National Bank of New York
Research-Cottrell, Inc.
The Research Institute of America, Inc.
Revlon, Inc.

Rexnord Inc.
Reynolds Metals Company
Richardson-Vicks, Inc.
Riviana Foods Inc.
Rockefeller Family & Associates
The Rockefeller Brothers Fund, Inc.
The Rockefeller Group
Rockwell International Corporation
Rohn and Haas Company
Rolling Thunder, Inc.
ROLM Corporation
Rolscreen Company
Rorer Group Inc.
Rospatch Corporation
Ross, Johnston & Kersting, Inc.
Royal Insurance
Rubbermaid Incorporated
RUST International Corporation
Ryco Division, Reilly-Whiteman, Inc.
SDS Biotech Corporation
SKF Industries, Inc.
SNET
SPS Technologies, Inc.
Safeco Insurance Company
Saga Corporation
The St. Paul Companies
Salomon Inc.
Sanders Associates, Inc.
Sandoz, Inc.
Santa Fe Southern Pacific Corporation
Sara Lee Corporation
Schering-Plough Corporation
Schlegel Corporation
Charles Schwab & Company Inc.
The Scott & Fetzer Company
Scott Paper Company
Seaboard System Railroad
Joseph E. Seagram & Sons, Inc.
Sealed Power Corporation
Sealright Company, Inc.
G. D. Searle & Company
Seattle Trust & Savings Bank
Security-Connecticut Life Insurance Company
Security Pacific Corporation
Security Van Lines, Inc.
Shell Oil Company
Sheller-Globe Corporation
Shenandoah Life Insurance Company

The Sherwin-Williams Company
Siemens Capital Corporation
Siemens Energy & Automation, Inc.
Sifco Industries, Inc.
Simpson Investment Company
Skinner Corporation
SmithKline Beckman Corporation
Society Bank, National Association
Sonat Inc.
Sony Corporation of America
Soo Line Railroad Company
South Carolina National Corporation
South Central Bell Telephone Company
Southern Bell
Southern Life Insurance Company
The Southland Corporation
South-Western Publishing Company
Sovran Financial Corporation
Spring Arbor Distribution Company
Springs Industries, Inc.
Squibb Corporation
The Stackpole Corporation
Stanadyne, Inc.
Standard Insurance Company
The Standard Oil Company
The Standard Products Company
Stanhome, Inc.
The Stanley Works
State Mutual Life Assurance Company of America
State Street Bank and Trust Company
Stauffer Chemical Company
Stearnes Catalytic World Corporation
Steiger Tractor, Inc.
Sterling Drug, Inc.
J. P. Stevens & Company, Inc.
Stone & Webster, Inc.
The Stop and Shop Companies, Inc.
Subaru of America, Inc.
Sun Company, Inc.
Sun Life Assurance Company of Canada
The Superior Oil Company
Swiss American Securities, Inc.
Syntex Corporation
TRW Inc.
Tambrands, Inc.
Tandy Corporation
Technimetrics, Inc.
Tektronix, Inc.
Tennant Company
Tenneco Inc.
Tesoro Petroleum Corporation
Texas Commerce Bank—Houston Foundation
Texas Eastern Corporation
Texas Gas Transmission Corporation
Texas Instruments Inc.
Textron Inc.
Thomas & Betts Corporation
J. Walter Thompson Company
TICOR
Time Inc.
The Times Journal Company
Times Mirror
Times Publishing Company and Congressional Quarterly, Inc.
The Toro Company
The Torrington Company
Total Petroleum (North America) Ltd.
Towers, Perrin, Forster & Crosby
Townsend & Bottum, Inc.
Toyota Motor Sales, U.S.A., Inc.
Trailer Train Company
The Trane Company
Transamerica Corporation
Transco Energy Company
The Travelers Corporation
Travelers Express Company, Inc.
Tremco Inc.
Trinova Corporation
Triskelion Ltd.
Trust Company Bank, Atlanta
The Turner Corporation
US West, Inc.
UGI Corporation
UNUM Life Insurance Company
US Air
USG Corporation
Union Bank
Union Camp Corporation
Union Electric Company
Union Mutual Fire Insurance Company
Union Pacific Corporation
Union Trust Company
United Bank of Denver, N. A.
United Engineers & Constructors, Inc.

United Gas Pipe Line
United Jersey Banks
United Mutual Savings Bank
United Parcel Service
United States Trust Company of
   New York
United States Tobacco Company
United States Leasing International,
   Inc.
United Technologies Corporation
United Telephone Company of
   Indiana, Inc.
United Telephone Company of
   Florida
United Telecommunications, Inc.
United Telephone Company of Ohio
United Virginia Bank
Unocal Corporation
The Upjohn Company
Urban Investment and Development
   Company
USLIFE Corporation
Utah International Inc.
Valero Energy Corporation
Varian Associates, Inc.
Vulcan Materials Company
The Wachovia Corporation/
   Wachovia Bank & Trust Company,
   N.A.
Warnaco

Warner-Lambert Company
Washington National Insurance
   Company
The Washington Post Company
Waste Management, Inc.
Watkins-Johnson Company
Wausau Insurance Companies
C. J. Webb, Inc.
Wells Fargo Bank, N.A.
West Point–Pepperell Foundation,
   Inc.
Western Publishing Company, Inc.
Westvaco Corporation
Whirlpool Corporation
Whittaker Corporation
John Wiley & Sons, Inc.
Willamette Industries, Inc.
Williams & Company, Inc.
Winn-Dixie Stores, Inc.
The Wiremold Company
Wisconsin Bell Inc.
Wisconsin Electric Power Company
Wolverine World Wide, Inc.
Wyman-Gordon Company
The Yankee Companies, Inc.
Yarway Corporation
Arthur Young
Young & Rubicam Inc.
Zapata Corporation
Zurn Industries, Inc.

Index

A

Aid to Families with Dependent Children (AFDC), 82
Alternative funding: search for, 1-2; variation of, 52-56. *See also* Revenue diversification; Revenue generation; Revenue source
Alumni, 2; relations with, 30-32; resources on, 85; as source of funds, 29-30; as volunteers, 32-33
American Federation of Small Business, 65
American Nurses' Association, 41, 43
Angel, D., 2, 7, 8, 9, 10, 12, 13, 14, 15
Arnold, A. D., 3
Aslanian, C. B., 37, 44

B

Baker, G. A., III, 23, 27
Barton, Stevens, and Massarsky, Ltd., 60, 66
Belmont Technical College, 53-54, 55
Betz, F., 37, 44
Blank, A. S., 25
Blocker, C. E., 37, 44
Breneman, D. W., 59, 66
Brightman, R. W., 3, 57, 66

C

Cable television, 3, 46-47
California, 58, 59; for-profit ventures in, 64-65; performance contracting in, 75; tax-exempt status in, 62-63. *See also* Proposition 13
Carnegie Council on Policy Issues in Higher Education, 57, 58, 66
Catanzaro, J. L., 3
Chand, S., 3
Child care, 55
Citrus College, 12-13
Clayton, P. C., 25, 26
Commercial development of land, 67-68; benefits from, 71-72; cautions on, 72-73; concept consideration in, 68-69; developer selection for, 70-71; development authority for, 69-70; financial considerations in, 71; plan formulation for, 69
Community college foundation(s), 2, 7; active 12; assets of, 10-11; establishment of, 11; history of, 8-9; resources on, 86-88, 92; revitalization example of, 12-13; success of, 11-12, 15-20. *See also* Foundations
Community colleges: commercial land development by, 67-73; contract training at, 37-44; for-profit activities of, 61-65; revenue diversification of, 60, 65-66; revenue situation of, 57-59
Companies. *See* Corporations
Compton College, 64
Computer-assisted design (CAD), 51
Computer-integrated manufacturing (CAM), 51
Continuing education, cosponsorships model for, 41-44
Continuing Education Center for Health Professionals (CECHP), 41-44; and Instructional Television Fixed Service, 47
Contract model, 39-41
Contract training, 2-3; contract model for, 39-40; cosponsorships model for, 41-44; EDI as, 38-39
Corporations: giving policies of, 86, 93-110; with matching policy, 111-120
Cosponsorships model, 41-44
Council for the Advancement and Support of Education (CASE), 15
Crowson, J., 10, 13-14
Curry, B. A., 3, 37, 44

D

DANTES (Defense Activity for Non-Traditional Education Support) catalogue, 80

121

Degerstedt, L. M., 8, 14
Delta College, 55
Distance learning, 45-46; cable network for, 46-47; Instructional Television Fixed Service for, 47; satellite video teleconferencing for, 47-49
Duffy, E. F., 11, 14

E

Economic development, 51-56
Edison State Community College, 54
Emory-Riddle Aeronautical University, 60
Employee Development Institute (EDI), 38-39; and cable television, 46-47
Endowed Teaching Chair Program, 2; and distinguished professors concept, 21-22; as motivator for contributors, 26-27; plan and organization of, 24-26; and Teaching/Learning Project, 23-24

F

Federal Economic Development Administration, 54
Fields, C., 52, 56
Fine, M., 25
Florida, alternative funding in, 53
Florida Academic Improvement Trust Fund (FAITF), 21, 22
Florida Community College at Jacksonville (FCCJ), performance contracting at, 75, 77, 78, 79-80, 81-83
For-profit activities, 3; criticisms of, 61-62; examples of, 64-65; organization of, 63-64; types of, 62-63
Foundations, 2; policies of, 93-110. *See also* Community college foundation(s)
Friedrich, O., 57, 66
Friends, alumni as, 29-33
Fund raising: resources on, 88-90, 91, 92; successful, 15-20

G

G.I. Bill of 1944, 37
Gares, D., 2, 7, 8, 9, 10, 12, 13, 14, 15
General Motors, 55

Gill, D., 25
Glandon, B. L., 12, 14
Goodyear Tire, 55
Government: and economic development, 3, 51-55; performance contracting for, 79-80; reduced expenditures by, 1, 58-59
Graham, F. R., 11, 14
Grants: Pell, 58; versus performance contracts, 76
Grinnell College, 60

H

Hall, J., 16
Heintzelman, K., 3
Heller, S., 23, 27
Herrmann, S. E., 2, 21, 27
Higher Education Act of 1965, 9, 22
Hollingsworth, P., 11, 12, 14
Hopkins, B., 61, 66

I

Institute for New Enterprise Development, 65
Instructional Television Fixed Service (ITFS), 3, 47
Internal Revenue Service, 9, 61; and nonprofit status, 62, 63, 64

J

Jackson, C., 3
Job Training Partnership Act (JTPA), 55, 76-77, 82

K

Katsinas, S. G., 2, 21, 27
Keener, B. J., 22, 27
Keeping America Working Project, 55
Kooi, J. B., 3, 45, 49

L

Lake County, College of, 55
Lakeland College Foundation, 7
Land. *See* Commercial development of land
Lestina, R., 3, 37, 44
Lindner, W. K., 3, 67, 73

Long Beach City College, 8
Luck, M. F., 8, 10, 14

M

McCabe, R. H., 25, 26
McDowell, R. W., 3, 67, 73
McKenney, J., 52
Maradian, S., 3, 51, 56
Massachusetts, alternative funding in, 52-53
Media delivery systems, 3. *See also* Cable television; Instructional Television Fixed Service (ITFS); Satellite video teleconferencing
Miami-Dade Community College, 7; Endowed Teaching Chair of, 21-27
Miami-Dade Community College Foundation, 22-23, 25
Mid-Metro Regional Development, Incorporated, 38
Midland College Foundation, 7
Midway Junior College, 8
Mingle, J. R., 58, 59, 66
Model: contract, 39-40; cosponsorships, 41-44; distance learning, 45-49

N

National Business League, 65
National Council for Resource Development, 15
National Council for Small Business Development, 65
National Home Study Council Guide, 80
National Trust for Historic Preservation, 54
Naylor, H. H., 33
Nelson, S. C., 59, 66
Nusz, P. J., 8, 14

O

Ohio, alternative funding in, 53-55
Oliver, J. G., 3, 75, 83
Orange Coast College, 64

P

Patrick Henry Community College Foundation, 7

Pell grants, 58
Performance contracts, 76; availability of, 76-77; developing proposals for, 80; at FCCJ, 79-80; flexibility and accountability of, 77-78; monitoring, 81; operation of, 78-79; problems with, 81-83; versus grants, 76
Plummer, R. H., 37, 44
Pokrass, R. J., 2, 29, 33
Powers, D. R., 37, 44
Powers, M. F., 37, 44
President's Blue Ribbon Committee, 26
Private Industry Council, 77, 79
Private sector, solicitation from, 15-20. *See also* Corporations
Profit. *See* For-profit activities
Proposition 13 (California), 12, 13

R

Rasmussen, P., 12, 13, 14
Reilley, T. A., 11, 14
Retrenchment, 58
Revenue diversification, 60, 65-66; for-profit activities for, 61-65
Revenue generation: contract model for, 39-40; cosponsorship model for, 41-44; distance learning model for, 45-49
Revenue source, commercial development of land as, 67-73. *See also* Alternative funding; Revenue diversification; Revenue generation
Richardson, R. C. Jr., 37, 44
Robison, S., 8, 12, 14
Roueche, J. E., 23, 27
Rowland, A. W., 29, 33
Ryan, G. J., 2, 3, 15, 16, 20

S

Santa Barbara Community College, 64
Santa Barbara Community College Foundation, 7
Satellite video teleconferencing, 47-49
Schoolcraft College, commercial development of land by, 3, 67-73
Schoolcraft Development Authority, 69, 71

Service Corps of Retired Executives (SCORE), 65
Sharron, W. H., Jr., 11, 12, 14, 15
Sinclair Community College, 55
Siskiyous, College of the, 65
Skidmore College, 60
Small Business Administration (SBA), 65
Smith, N., 16
Smith, N. J., 15, 17, 18, 20
Social security benefits, 58
Southern Regional Education Board, 58
Spair, D., 3
Spence, C. C., 3, 75, 83
Stanford, 60
Statistic process control (SPC), 51
Success: of foundations, 11-12; in fund raising, 15-20; resources on, 85-86, 90-91
Supplemental Educational Opportunity Grants, 58-59

T

Taxes, 9, 62-63
Teaching, and fund raising, 2. See also Endowed Teaching Chair Program
Teaching/Learning Project, 23-24
Teaching/Learning Project 1986-87 Summary Report, 24, 27

Technology, media, 45-49
Technology training, 51-55
Teleconferencing, 3. See also Satellite video teleconferencing
Thomas Edison programs, 55
Thor, L. M., 75, 83
Tolle, D. J., 10, 14
Traylor, H. J., 2, 21, 27
Triton College: contract training at, 38-40; cosponsorships model at, 41-44; distance learning at, 45-49
Tyler Junior College, 54-55

U

U.S. Department of Defense, 55, 79-80
United Steelworkers of America, 54, 55

V

Video teleconferencing. See Satellite video teleconferencing

W

Walters, L., 11, 14
Wattenbarger, J. L., 11, 14, 22, 27
Williams, R. M., 60, 62, 66
Willing Founders Program, 25-26
Wilson, M., 33
Wisconsin, University of, 60
Wolfson, L., III, 25

U.S. Postal Service
STATEMENT OF OWNERSHIP, MANAGEMENT AND CIRCULATION
Required by 39 U.S.C. 3685

1A. Title of Publication	1B. PUBLICATION NO.	2. Date of Filing
New Directions for Community Colleges	1 2 1 - 7 1 0	10/27/89

3. Frequency of Issue	3A. No. of Issues Published Annually	3B. Annual Subscription Price
quarterly	4	$48 individual $64 institutional

4. Complete Mailing Address of Known Office of Publication *(Street, City, County, State and ZIP+4 Code) (Not printers)*
350 Sansome Street, San Francisco, CA 94104-1310

5. Complete Mailing Address of the Headquarters of General Business Offices of the Publisher *(Not printer)*
(above address)

6. Full Names and Complete Mailing Address of Publisher, Editor, and Managing Editor *(This item MUST NOT be blank)*
Publisher *(Name and Complete Mailing Address)*
Jossey-Bass Inc., Publishers (above address)

Editor *(Name and Complete Mailing Address)*
Arthur Cohen, ERIC, 8118 Math Sciences Bldg., UCLA, Los Angeles, CA 90024

Managing Editor *(Name and Complete Mailing Address)*
Steven Piersanti, President, Jossey-Bass Inc., Publishers (above address)

7. Owner *(If owned by a corporation, its name and address must be stated and also immediately thereunder the names and addresses of stockholders owning or holding 1 percent or more of total amount of stock. If not owned by a corporation, the names and addresses of the individual owners must be given. If owned by a partnership or other unincorporated firm, its name and address, as well as that of each individual must be given. If the publication is published by a nonprofit organization, its name and address must be stated.) (Item must be completed.)*

Full Name	Complete Mailing Address
Maxwell Communications Corp., plc	Headington Hill Hall Oxford OX30BW U.K.

8. Known Bondholders, Mortgagees, and Other Security Holders Owning or Holding 1 Percent or More of Total Amount of Bonds, Mortgages or Other Securities *(If there are none, so state)*

Full Name	Complete Mailing Address
none	

9. For Completion by Nonprofit Organizations Authorized To Mail at Special Rates *(DMM Section 423.12 only)*
The purpose, function, and nonprofit status of this organization and the exempt status for Federal income tax purposes *(Check one)*

[ ] Has Not Changed During Preceding 12 Months
[ ] Has Changed During Preceding 12 Months
(If changed, publisher must submit explanation of change with this statement.)

10. Extent and Nature of Circulation	Average No. Copies Each Issue During Preceding 12 Months	Actual No. Copies of Single Issue Published Nearest to Filing Date
A. Total No. Copies *(Net Press Run)*	1900	2042
B. Paid and/or Requested Circulation		
1. Sales through dealers and carriers, street vendors and counter sales	112	49
2. Mail Subscription *(Paid and/or requested)*	885	944
C. Total Paid and/or Requested Circulation *(Sum of 10B1 and 10B2)*	997	993
D. Free Distribution by Mail, Carrier or Other Means Samples, Complimentary, and Other Free Copies	165	210
E. Total Distribution *(Sum of C and D)*	1162	1203
F. Copies Not Distributed		
1. Office use, left over, unaccounted, spoiled after printing	738	839
2. Return from News Agents		
G. TOTAL *(Sum of E, F1 and 2—should equal net press run shown in A)*	1900	2042

11. I certify that the statements made by me above are correct and complete

Signature and Title of Editor, Publisher, Business Manager, or Owner
Vice-President

PS Form 3526, Feb. 1989